GOOD TOYS

Debbie Wager
Judy Nygren

PANDA MONIUM BOOKS

© National Press, Inc. 1986
7508 Wisconsin Avenue
Bethesda, Maryland 20814
(301) 657-1616

Cover design by Barry Moyer.

Library of Congress Cataloging-in-Publication Data

Wager, Debbie, 1938–
    Good toys.

    1. Toys. I. Nygren, Judy, 1937–   . II. Title.
TS2301.T7W34 1986   688.7'2   86–23631
ISBN 0–915765–34–9

Dedication

To every child, teacher, parent and grandparent: We hope that you will benefit from this book.

Acknowledgments

The authors thank all of the teachers at the Clara Barton Center for their assistance, with special thanks to Eve Pines. We appreciate the efforts of Lowen's toy store in Bethesda, Maryland, the National Association for the Education of Young Children and Dr. Kathleen Miller.

Table of Contents

Chapter One

Introduction

This is a guidebook for buying safe, durable and enjoyable toys that will serve your children faithfully. Since there are thousands of new toys introduced each year, and since there are more than 100,000 toys on the market, this book does not attempt to review all toys.

While we are primarily writing about toys available on the market, it is a good idea to remember that all toys are not bought in a toy store. Besides making their own toys from ordinary household items such as yarn, fabric, cardboard boxes and so forth, children often find good toys in kitchen cupboards. Pots, pans, measuring cups and spoons, plastic bowls and muffin tins are good toys your children will enjoy playing with.

In addition to describing and discussing good toys, we have attempted to explain how toys should be selected. Traditional toys, "fad" toys and toys for children of different ages are all discussed. We have particularly noted those toys that will not go out of style because they are durable, stimulating and fun to use again and again.

Good Toys

Throughout this book we have used two symbols, a ✪ and a ▲. The ✪ denotes those toys that are basic toys for every household. If you can only buy one type of a particular category of toys make sure that it is marked with a ✪. The ▲ symbol indicates those toys recommended for day care centers.

Good toys are not necessarily expensive, although some may be. Buying toys that will be used and enjoyed for many years, even if they are somewhat costly, is a reasonable and sensible investment for your child's development.

Good toys are like good tools; children need good toys just as a cook or a carpenter needs good tools to make something. Play is children's work. It is the way in which they experiment with and learn about their world.

Toys can be made from discarded cups, mirrors, yarn, leftover material and cardboard boxes.

Toy Shopping Checklist

As you read this book keep in mind the fundamentals of good toys. All of these fundamentals are discussed in detail in this book. When you are shopping for toys ask yourself the following five basic questions:

1. Is the toy **safe** for the child who will be using it?

2. Will the toy be **used** over and over again?

3. Is the toy **durable** enough to withstand vigorous play?

4. Is the toy **challenging**?

5. Is the toy right for my child's level of **ability**?

1. Is the toy safe for the child who will be using it?

Safe toys are also well-made toys. Toys that come apart to expose sharp edges or points are dangerous. Safe toys are made with non-toxic materials and paints which are lead-free. Safe toys are shatter-proof. Safe toys for young children are not electric or battery operated. Electric toys can shock children and young children may chew on batteries.

The safety of a given toy depends on the child's age. A toy marked for a child of more than three years may contain small parts which an infant could swallow and choke on. An example of this was in the news recently. McDonald's restaurants gave out Lego and Duplo block sets with their "happy meals." Both of these toys are excellent toys **for children of specified ages**. However, McDonald's gave out Lego toys to children under three years of age. These toys contained small parts which several toddlers swallowed. Luckily none of the toddlers was severely harmed.

2. Will the toy be used over and over again?

A good toy is one that is used often and for many years. The key question to ask is "will the toy be fun for my child to play with?" If the toy is fun to play with your child will use it. A beautiful, safe and durable toy that is left on the shelf is not a good toy. Ask yourself "will my child be interested in playing with the toy when it is no longer new?"

Can the toy grow with your child? Certain toys, like interlocking blocks, can be played with by infants as well as six year olds. This is because blocks can be used in an infinite variety of ways. The same thing is true for paint sets and crayons.

3. Is the toy durable?

Durable toys are not necessarily indestructible toys. It is helpful, however, if the toy can be easily repaired. Some plastic toys cannot be repaired. Wooden toys are not easily broken, but can be glued if necessary. See chapter twelve for information about repairing toys and replacing toy pieces.

4. Is the toy challenging?

The key questions for this criterion is:

☐ Does the toy permit my child to be creative?

☐ Will the toy challenge him to devise solutions?

☐ Will it expand my child's cognitive or physical skills?

A toy can develop coordination and creativity; it can enhance a child's understanding of nature, people and places.

You should maintain a balance in the toys selected for your children between the more creative toys, such as building sets and design blocks that can be used in a number of different ways, and toys that tend to limit or define play, such as electronic toys.

5. Is the toy right for my child's level of ability?

A toy can be frustrating if it is too difficult, or it may be ignored because it is too simple. A toy should be challenging to your child, but not too challenging or it becomes frustrating.

Limits of this Book

There are, of course, some wonderful playthings that we have not been able to include because of space limitations. In our efforts to discuss toys and games in depth, we have excluded records and books. Books are probably one of the finest and most treasured items that you can buy your child but would have encompassed a volume by themselves.

Parents as Playmates

Let us not forget, as we think about the toys that children will enjoy, that the pleasure of playing with toys is enhanced by your participation in play. You, as the child's parent and friend, can show the child how to play with toys, how to share and how to learn from others. Your participation gives the child a good foundation for independent play and for play with other children. And your child will not be the only one who has a good time.

Alternative Sources for Toys

Most of the toys described in this book are available at good toy stores. This book describes in chapter ten many toys that can easily be made at home. Another good source for toys is catalog companies, especially for toys needed by child care facilities. The following catalog companies are sources for many good toys:

Beckley—Cardy
114 Gaither Drive
Mt. Laurel, NJ 08054
(800) 257-8338

Chaselle, Inc.
9645 Gerwig Lane
Columbia, MD 21046
(800) CHASELLE

Community Playthings
Route 213
Rifton, NY 12471
(914) 658-3141

Childcraft
20 Kilmer Road
P.O. Box 3081
Edison, NJ 08818
(800) 631-5652

World Wide Games
Colchester, CT 06415
(203) 537-2325

Introduction

Community Playthings makes all their toys, tricycles and classroom furniture of the highest quality. They will replace any parts that wear out.

World Wide Games make very handsome wooden games, such a skittles, backgammon and Chinese checkers.

Chapter Two

Safe Toys

Toys Can Hurt Children!

In the United States in 1985 there were approximately 123,000 injuries from toys which required emergency room treatment, according to the Consumer Product Safety Commission. About one quarter of those injuries were serious enough to require hospitalization.

These injuries represent only a small fraction of all injuries caused by toys because the figures do not include injuries that were treated by private doctors, or those treated at home. Injuries from bicycles and BB guns are not counted as toy injuries.

Injuries from toys can be very serious, even deadly. In 1984 thirty-three children died from toy-related injuries in the United States. According to the CPSC children under three are the most frequent victims of killer toys and choking is the most common cause of death.

Safe Toys

Balloons have caused many deaths by choking, including those of children up to age nine.

What You Can Do to Make Sure a Toy is Safe?

Whatever children can do with a toy, they **will do**. They will throw toys and use them to hit other children. Anticipate this and show your child how a toy should be used. **Watch out for:**

- ☐ sharp points
- ☐ projectiles
- ☐ small parts
- ☐ cords and strings
- ☐ loud noises
- ☐ electrical toys

Sharp Points

Even a safe toy can become dangerous when it is broken, if the pieces have jagged edges or sharp points. Broken toys can also expose dangerous prongs. We once found an adorable teddy bear whose nose pulled off on the very first try. What came out was not just a small piece of hard plastic that could have been swallowed easily, but the object that had held the nose—a rusty metal disc with two sharp metal prongs. That innocent teddy bear could have been lethal! This stuffed animal had been imported from the Far East, and it probably had been sitting in a damp warehouse near a dock, which caused the rusting.

We have found spinning tops with easily removed bases that revealed two and one-half inch long spikes, a skill game with a "magic wand" that could put out an eye, play "food" toys with tin foil covers that were so sturdy that they formed a sharp edge that could cut a child and a toy tool set with a metal, realistic-looking saw and other tools with very sharp edges.

Projectiles

Projectiles are propelled objects—guided or unguided missiles, toy guns that shoot corks, plastic bullets and disks. These can be turned into weapons that hurt and maim children. The most vulnerable part of a child's body, and the most commonly injured from projectiles is the eyes.

At least one child has died as a result of detonating live firearm ammunition in a toy gun, and several children have died swallowing projectiles.

There have been countless "near misses." Several years ago a young boy placed a small rocketship toy in his mouth. The rocket did not belong there but then children often do surprising things with their toys. Because the "triggers" were toward the rear of the rocketship he was able to reach them, pressing down to shoot. The rocket was released with such force that it lodged in the boy's throat, and he began to choke. A quick trip to the nearby emergency room saved his life.

The manufacturer promptly took the toy off the market and redesigned the spaceship so that the projectile levers were in the front part of the spaceship. That way, if the rocket were inside a child's mouth, his hands would not be able to reach the levers to launch it.

Children should not be permitted to play with adult lawn darts or adult dart sets. Any arrows or darts used by children should have soft cork tips, rubber suction cups or other protective tips intended to prevent injury. Never let children use the metal darts with long points that are available in many toy stores.

Small Parts

Toys that are good and safe for older children, like construction sets that have many small pieces, can be extremely dangerous in the hands of infants. Often when a toy is labeled "for ages three and over" or "not intended for use by children under three," it means that there are parts small enough to choke a small child.

Make sure that rattles, squeakers and teething toys are too large to fit entirely into a baby's mouth. Check again after you have tried compressing the toy. Make sure that the squeaker cannot be removed from the toy. Check the seams of stuffed animals and dolls: if they are not tight, small pellets that make up the stuffing could be swallowed or become lodged in a child's ear or nose.

Cords and Strings

Never buy toys with long strings, loops or cords for young children. The cords could accidentally become wrapped around a baby's neck and strangle him.

Good Toys

Recently, two children died after they were strangled by a string connected to a crib toy. See chapter three concerning safe crib toys.

Do not tie strings to pacifiers! These cords could accidentally get caught on a doornob or crib post and choke your child. The Consumer Product Safety Commission has banned a pacifier sold with an attached cord.

Loud Noises

Toy cap guns can cause sound loud enough to damage hearing! No cap gun should be fired closer than one foot from the ear, nor should it be fired indoors. Toy guns are not good toys, but if you cannot resist your child's pressure to buy them, buy the quietest ones available. Loud toys, besides driving parents crazy, can cause hearing loss.

Electrically Operated Toys

Electrical toys can shock and burn your children. Do not buy an electrical toy for a child who is too young to use it. Children under age five should never use electrical toys. Depending on the child, electrical toys should be avoided, sometimes until age eight.

Electrical toys should be carefully inspected. Look for tattered cords, broken parts and exposed wires.

When buying battery-operated toys make sure that the battery cover is secure. Battery covers often open unintentionally. Small children chew on batteries which contain dangerous chemicals. Keep an eye on your toddler when he or she is playing with a battery operated toy.

Dangerous Toy Hotline

If you find a dangerous toy being sold you should notify the CPSC by calling their toll-free hotline:

800-638-CPSC

Your examination of toys for hazards could uncover a dangerous toy that was missed by government testers. The CPSC cannot test every toy on the market: there are too many toys and not enough inspectors. One of the goals of this book is to create an army of informed parents and grandparents who will inspect toys for hazards to save their children and grandchildren from unsuspected dangers.

Chapter Three

Durable Toys

Durable toys are often more expensive initially but their lasting qualities more than compensate for their original purchase cost. Well-made toys, as well as being more durable, often tend to be more attractive and better designed. In addition their durability benefits the child by sparing him from the disappointment and frustration of broken toys. These toys have more eye-appeal for the parent and for the child. These are toys that become a child's old friends.

In general, toys that are constructed of wood are more durable than their counterparts constructed in plastic. However, because wooden toys are heavier than plastic ones, infants and toddlers may be better off with plastic toys. Avoid purchasing lightweight plastic

Durable Toys

toys which can break apart at the seams when stepped on.

Best Toys

Looking at toys over the past twenty years, we see that certain toys have retained their popularity. These toys are not only durable but have withstood changes in style and taste.

There are many ways to categorize toys. We have come up with ten useful categories. Just as our diet should include the four basic food groups, a good toy collection should include toys from each of these basic groups.

The basic toy categories are:

☐ Manipulative Toys

☐ Building Systems

☐ Imaginative Playthings

☐ Expressive/Creative Toys

☐ Arts and Crafts

☐ Mathematical Concept Toys

☐ Exploring/Discovering Toys

☐ Musical Toys

☐ Sports

☐ Games

Good Toys

Manipulative Toys

Manipulative Toys include many primary toys such as blocks, puzzles and sorting toys. These toys allow a child to develop coordination between the eye and hand and improve fine motor skills. Blocks, of which there are many types, can be used to build things. They are closely related to the next category of toys.

Building Systems

Building Systems are usually interlocking sets for making buildings, cars and other objects. Lincoln Logs, Legos, Duplos, Bristle Blocks and Construx are examples of this type of toy. In addition to developing motor skills these toys encourage creativity, experimentation and decision-making.

Imaginative Playthings

Imaginative Playthings include dolls, dollhouses, train sets, play villages and medical kits. These toys allow children to use their imaginations and to act out different social roles.

Expressive/Creative Toys

Expressive/creative toys allow childen to experiment with line, color and shape to express their own creative ideas, within limits set by the toys. Etch-a-Sketch is an example of this type of toy.

Durable Toys

Arts and Crafts

Arts and crafts materials are expressive and creative as well. However, they are different from expressive/creative toys because they are materials, not toys. Arts and crafts materials give children wide creative latitude.

Mathematical Concept Toys

Mathematical concept toys are sets which teach children about relationships between different size objects, numbers of objects and other mathematical concepts.

Musical Toys

Musical toys are small-sized musical instruments that allow children to play music and create sounds.

Sports Toys

Sports toys teach children how to use their minds and bodies to reach a goal. They also teach playing by the rules, sportsmanship, winning and losing and many other concepts.

Games

Games teach children many of the things that they learn by sports, such as winning and losing, reaching a goal and so forth. Games are usually less physical than sports, and usually involve more mental skills. Games form a broad category which ranges from word games,

Good Toys

to card games, board games and electronic games.

Keep Your Child Balanced

By exposing your child to many types of toys you will not only keep your child busy but will keep his skills and interests balanced. Toys are for pleasure as well as for learning. By playing with a wide variety of toys your child will have a better chance of finding ones that he likes and uses. Toys that are not used are not good toys.

Test Driving Toys

Toy libraries are like libraries for books except that you check out toys instead. Nearly every major city has a toy library. See chapter eleven which explains how these libraries operate and how they can be found. Toy libraries allow you to try out a toy before purchasing it. You can observe whether your child likes to play with a particular toy before you are committed to paying for it.

Chapter Four

Toys as Fashion

As with products made for adults, toys of different types come in and go out of fashion. And often those fashions are dictated by millions of dollars worth of television advertising. Children want to be the first on their block to have a new something or other just as their parents want to have a piece of jewelry or the "in" car or dress.

You are not going to stop your children from wanting to possess these new, trendy toys. And trendy, fashionable toys are not necessarily bad toys. However these toys can dominate a toy collection and make it unbalanced. Also many of these trendy toys are very expensive. By spending a large amount on one toy, or one type of toy, you may not be spending from your toy budget as wisely as you should.

Certain toys have retained their appeal and use for many years. They have withstood changes in style and taste, and have endured through the passing fancies and fads in toys. Trendy toys, which surface each season, tend to be replaced by a new set of trendy toys the next season.

The top ten selling toys in the United States for late 1986, compiled by **Toy & Hobby World Magazine** were:

1. Pound Puppies.

2. G.I. Joe.

3. Barbie.

4. MASK (Mobile Army Strike Kommand).

5. Transformers.

6. Cabbage Patch Kids.

7. Teddy Ruxpin.

8. Mad Balls.

9. WWF Wrestlers.

10. Jem.

Because toy fashions change, many of these ten toys will not appear on the 1987 toy list. Some of them will. Barbie dolls have been on the list for decades.

It's Gotta Have a Gimmick

To paraphrase an old song, "it's got to have a gimmick" seems to be the by-word of much of the toy industry today. What we find most disturbing about the dolls and stuffed animals on shelves of toy stores is the focus on gimmickry. One sees very few simple, basic playthings—everything walks or talks or moves. We think that it is important to ask ourselves what a toy signifies for a child and what needs a toy satisfies in his life.

Take the example of the ordinary teddy bear: one who does nothing but look cuddly and remain available to be slept with, dragged about, talked to and hugged. This basic teddy bear serves an important function for the young child. It provides him with a sense of comfort and security. In loving and caring for his teddy bear, the child practices his loving and caring skills. It is a transitional object which helps the child in his task of separating himself emotionally from his primary caregivers.

The child's fantasies while he is playing with the teddy bear allow him to try out some of the complex feelings, fears and ideas he is experiencing as he develops a sense of identity. The simple, basic teddy bear permits the child to work on those developmentally appropriate tasks which are a natural part of growing up.

However, what happens when we start adding gimmicks to our basic, lovable teddy bear? For example, take a teddy bear whose arms open and shut. This feature would not significantly intrude on the stuffed animal's primary function. Arms which open and shut are inviting. The bear still can be used in the classic ways to provide satisfaction for the child.

Now, let's make the bear talk and blink his eyes. The teddy bear is now something to look at and to listen to. Instead of the child imagining what the bear is saying, the teddy bear does its own talking. How well this bear serves the child depends on how much talking and blinking distract or involve the child apart from his desire to hold and hug his teddy bear.

Finally, let's add a cassette player to teddy. Now the teddy bear is a music maker and story teller. This is no longer just a teddy bear. He is a heavy, clumsy entertainment center.

We do not mean to criticize all of these interactive toys. For example, Teddy Ruxpin's synchronized animation is fascinating to children, and the books and tapes made for him are well done. But Teddy Ruxpin is not a plain old teddy bear.

It becomes necessary as you make your toy-buying decisions to understand what you intend to buy your child. Is your intention to provide him with a teddy bear or to entertain him? If you want to buy an entertainment center for your child you can find other toys which are a better value. You must be sure that you are not confusing high-tech gimmicks which are intriguing, with those qualities which make a toy satisfying for a child.

We have found too many high-tech, gimmicky toys to be unsatisfying and unused. Will the child play with it for a week or a month and then grow tired of it? Will this year's expensive Christmas toy still be around next year? Ask yourself, is the robot, or teddy bear a high-tech gimmick, or is it a good toy that your child will play with and enjoyed for years to come?

Restrictive Nature of "Status" Toys

One "high status" toy among the preschool set is

the action figure, or super-hero doll, including Super-man, He-Man, MASK and Tranformer figures. These toys are most often derived from television shows. The action figures are a good examples of toys, the mere possession of which, virtually guarantees friends and ad-mirers.

There is no question that these figures are extremely appealing to young children. They represent the power to alter circumstances, an ability which children wish they possessed. Children, who are small and relatively powerless in their worlds of home and school, crave, on a fantasy level, the power to control their environment. Play with these heroic figures with superhuman strength, gives children tremendous emotional satisfac-tion. It allows them to ease, however briefly, their fears for their safety and satisfies their desire to have control over their environment.

These toys are not necessarily bad for children. The characters, in general, fight for good causes and use their powers to protect the rights and safety of others. However their success is usually achieved through phys-ical force rather than by intelligence and discussion, the means by which rational adults solve their problems.

For boys, in particular, who often have very active aggressive fantasies, these action figures serve to permit the aggression to be played out in an acceptable manner. In addition these action figures may serve as the only "dolls" that boys allow themselves to play with. As dolls they leave something to be desired, but they can be dressed (some in battle armor), made to walk and talk as one would an ordinary doll.

For all these reasons, these toys are very compelling

to children. However, the action doll is, to a great extent, a very restrictive toy. These toys are usually played with in a limited number of ways. By the very nature of the television shows or movies from which they derive, limits are imposed on play. Children play out the stories that they have seen on television, rather than stories which arise out of their own lives or imaginations. They play with only those characters identified in the television story.

One of the problems for girls who may wish to join in play is that few of these superhero figures are female. The following example demonstrates both the restrictive nature of these figures and the fact that there are few female super-human figures: Ten five year olds (five girls and five boys) were playing with Star Wars characters. Each boy could play a character, but the girls had a problem, which nearly eliminated all but one of them from playing the game. There is only one female character in Star Wars, Princess Leia. Fortunately, the group was creative enough to invent other female characters, Princess Leia's sister, cousin, friend and next-door neighbor.

Not all children are as ingenious as this. Instead they lock themselves into playing the parts of only those characters identified in the story.

Playing "house" by contrast has an endless cast of male and female characters with a variable story line depending on the ideas and thought of the children who are participating.

While it may be difficult to avoid buying these types of toys, we advise you to limit the number of them that you acquire. Because they are restrictive toys and

Toys as Fashion

because they are so appealing to children, it is important to make sure that children have alternative toys
which you encourage them to play with.

Programmed Toys

Both gimmicky toys and restrictive toys can be
considered "programmed toys." They are programmed in
different ways. Some gimmicky toys have computer
chips in them which program their behavior. Some
so-called action figures are programmed by the
television shows or movies that bring them to life. In
both cases the toy restricts free and creative play.

This is not to say that if you buy programmed toys
that you will have programmed children. We mention
these theories and concepts so that you will think
about the toys that you buy and the reasons that you
are buying them. Please keep in mind that a toy collection should be balanced, and that children should be
exposed to all types of toys. We should strive to limit
the "status" and "fad" toys as we should limit our
children's intake of junk food. Although children are at-
tracted to french fries and candy, a diet limited to
those items will not be healthy for the child. Parents
should strive to give their children a balanced diet of
toys.

Chapter Five

Crib and Playpen Toys

Babies are not all alike. Differences in temperament show up soon after birth. Some newborns seem to sleep all the time while others are active and awake more than their parents thought possible.

Monitor Your Infant at All Times

If you do not have an intercom in your home, you should buy a portable intercom for your baby's room. Fisher-Price makes a good one called **Nursery Monitor.** Basically this is an intercom without the expense or installation normally associated with it. This high-quality device allows parents and babysitters to listen in on a sleeping or playing infant while in another part of the house. With use of this device you will be alerted immediately should your child experience a toy-related, or any other type of accident or emergency.

What Toys Will Stimulate a Newborn Baby?

In the very beginning of life the newborn cannot yet

focus his eyes, but he can respond to light and to sounds. By the time your child is one month old, he can stare happily at colorful objects that move and can be soothed by music. Because of this, a good first toy purchase is a **crib mobile,** which provides both visual and aural stimulation.

Crib Mobiles

Crib mobiles are hanging objects that are suspended from a bar which is attached to the side of the crib. The objects move, either by a breeze or by a wind-up mechanism. **A word of caution:** mobiles should be within eye range but out of reach. And wonderful as they are, mobiles should be removed from the crib when your baby begins to sit up. A sitting baby can pull down the mobile and injure himself.

The Dancing Animals Music Box Mobile, by Fisher-Price, has four colorful, soft vinyl animals angled to face the baby while he is lying on his back. The wind-up music box plays Brahm's Lullabye for ten minutes, which often can help your baby go to sleep. There is an on/off switch and a clamp which easily attaches to a crib or shelf.

Lullabye Rainbow, by Tomy, fits across the crib, rail-to-rail, in the shape of an arc. There is no need to remove it because it automatically adjusts when the rail is lowered. The colorful musical unit travels slowly from side to side while the sun peeks in and out of the cloud and its eyes open and close. A basket and balloon twirl while music plays.

Mirrors

No one can resist looking at himself in a mirror—and newborn babies are no exception. Even though he probably cannot recognize it as "himself," the baby will still be fascinated by what he sees: a colorful object that moves. A **Big Bird Mirror** is shown below:

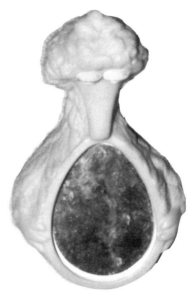

Naturally, baby mirrors are never made of glass, so they won't break if dropped or bumped into. **Baby's First Mirror,** by Johnson & Johnson, is a shatterproof, high-resolution, acrylic mirror housed in a sturdy 13 inch plastic frame. This mirror easily attaches to a crib, playpen or wall.

Another good mirror is **Peek 'N See Mirror,** by Playskool.

Crib Gyms

We deleted recommendations on crib gyms because

many toy safety experts believe that all crib gyms are unsafe.

Music Boxes

Music boxes are good crib toys for three month olds. They soothe and amuse. Music boxes come hidden in animals, in boxes and in other forms which either attach to the crip or are free-standing.

Pull—A—Byes, by Tomy, easily attaches to cribs and door handles and plays for 80 seconds. **Music Box Moon**, by Fisher-Price plays "When You Wish Upon a Star" while the moon rocks, creating a twinkling star effect with nighttime graphics on the screen.

Stuffed Toys

Stuffed toys are ageless. For newborns and very young babies choose stuffed toys that are washable, flame-resistant and non-toxic. A good stuffed animal can withstand lots of loving and squeezing. Musical stuffed animals make wonderful toys, but the musical mechanism makes the toy less cuddly. Probably the best overall quality stuffed animals are made by Stieff, a West German company in business for generations. Dakin mades a quality product for a moderate price as does Eden, Gund and Kamar.

Rattles

Rattles have been around for centuries. They were first designed to ward off evil spirits and even then could distract or amuse a cranky child. Used in small doses rattles can entertain and stimulate. Good rattles are easy to grasp and are fully washable as they will get dirty and babies will put them up to their mouths.

There are lots of rattles on the market made of a variety of materials, including plastic, wood and cloth.

Wrist Jingles, by Playskool, are soft, fabric rattles that attach around baby's wrist or ankle with Velcro fasteners. They are machine washable and dryer-safe. Wrist Jingles are ideal for young babies who are unable to hold a rattle.

One Ring Circus, by Fisher-Price, is a colorful rattle with a wide, strong strap which attaches easily and securely to strollers, highchairs and other surfaces.

Tracking Tube and **Wiggle Worm**, by Johnson & Johnson, are more than just rattles. Tracking Tube has a red liquid blob inside the clear handlebar, which slowly moves from handle to handle, encouraging the infant to follow the blob. The rattle is in one handle and a squeaker is in the other. Wiggle Worm has a brightly colored cloth body with rattles, a tail that crackles, a teether and a squeaker. It is machine washable and dryer-safe. **Note**: all Johnson & Johnson toys come with a 16 page booklet for parents, outlining child development at different ages. This booklet helps parents understand what skills the toys help build at each stage of development and includes a toll-free telephone number for questions and comments. Wiggle Worm is shown on the next page:

Crib Toys

Teething Rings

Teething rings come in a wide assortment of materials, shapes, colors and prices. Good ones are washable, durable and easy to hold. Monitor your child's use of teething devices closely. If the teething ring cracks or breaks, throw it away.

First Balls

Chime Ball, by Fisher-Price is an old standard. It is a large, colorful, plastic weighted ball that rolls, chimes and floats.

Clutch Balls, by Creative Playthings, have irregular surfaces. Their indentations and ridges form handles, making it easier for baby to grip and carry. Creative Playthings' clutch balls are made in soft, flexible rubber. Other companies make similar products out of brightly colored cloth.

Activity Toys

At approximately six months the baby is sitting up—a milestone in his development and a signal that he is ready for a whole new series of toys. At this stage,

37

Good Toys

babies like toys that can **do** something—and they can do something **to**. These are **cause and effect** toys.

Remember: take away the mobile when your baby sits up. Replace it with an activity toy that attaches to the crib. The following are good activity toys that have been popular with parents and babies for years:

Busy Box, by Playskool, is a classic activity toy for infants that rewards the baby with ten different push, turn, spin and ring gadgets. It comes with a built-in, shatterproof mirror and attaches to any crib or playpen with safety straps.

The Activity Center, by Fisher-Price, also has ten different manipulative activities: push a button and a bell rings, turn a knob and characters go around, pull down a sqeaker, turn a phone dial and hear a clicking sound. It attaches to the sides of the crib.

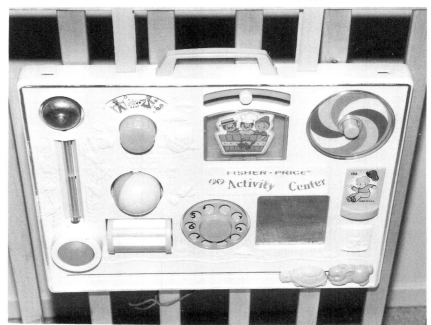

Crib Toys

Busy Poppin' Pals, by Child Guidance, is one of the best toys ever made. There are five different hand-eye coordination exercises—push, pull, turn, slide and rotate—all in a colorful, hard-plastic case.

Disney Musical Busy Box, by Playskool, is big and colorful and features a wind-up music box that twirls a bright bouquet of flowers as it plays a nursery melody. There are ten well-spaced manipulative activities. A flexible clamp attaches the busy box to the crib or playpen supporting the toy on its own. It is a very good play value.

Cloth Blocks

Cloth blocks are a good choice at age six months. The new **Learning Curves Color Cubes,** by Panosh Place, are soft, brightly decorated blocks which have pictures, letters and numbers on them. Each block makes a different sound: a rattle, a jingle or a click-clack. Velcro on several sides makes stacking or attaching them together very easy.

Stacking Toys

○ **Rock–A–Stack,** by Fisher-Price, has five plastic donut-shaped plastic rings of different sizes and colors, which fit over a dowel in sequence of size.

○ **Stack 'N Store Nesting Cubes,** by Little Tykes, are large, strong and colorful. The five separate pieces can be stacked to build a tower 20 inches high. The cubes can also nest inside of each other or serve as a storage container for crayons. Playskool makes a similar set in a smaller size.

Activity Blocks, by Fisher-Price are four colorful, stacking and nesting blocks. Each block has its own special feature: a squeaker, beads that disappear, a clicking bird or a multicolored roller.

Balls in a Bowl, by Johnson & Johnson, consists of three see-through plastic balls of varying sizes that fit into each other. Each contains fluttering, reflective spinners. The toy is simple, yet versatile, and teaches the concepts of dropping, dumping and inside and outside.

Rings and Rollers, by Johnson & Johnson, has three colorful rings, and two clear stacks where colorful beads spiral down inside the roller. Each ring has a rattle, and all can be stacked together to create a colorful tower.

Bath Toys

In the tub, children love to play with empty plastic squirt bottles from dishwashing soap, measuring cups, funnels, small plastic bottles and jars with lids. Many household items serve as wonderful bath toys.

Coloroo Zoo creatures, by Mattel, look like ordinary stuffed animals, but are not. Place the cuddly creatures in warm water and they change color. Put them in cool water and they change back. The Coloroo Zoo also has hand puppets for the tub.

Tub Fun, by Fisher-Price, is a soft activity center that easily attaches to bathtub or tile with large suction cups. It has a sprinkler cup, a water wheel, squirter fish, a water buoy that toots, a pouring boat and a soft starfish. All of these items store on or in the fabric panel which is machine washable and dryer safe.

Safety Whale by several manufacturers, though not a toy, deserves special mention. A soft-rubber whale, which fits over the bathtub faucet, prevents children from getting scalded or bruised. It fits standard faucets or can be cut to fit.

Bath Activity Set, by Duplo, is a colorful and varied toy for infant tub play. Children can also play with standard Duplo blocks in the tub.

Bath Bubbles and **Ernie's Rubber Duckie**, both by Playskool are good bath toys. Bath bubbles are small, clear balls that have flutters inside and float. Ernie's Rubber Duckie is a **Sesame Street** toy that children love.

Chapter Six

Toys for Toddlers (Under Age Three)

Pre-nursery school children are making great strides in language, motor skills and in logic. Some are real dynamos—on the go every minute, up and down stairs, running around and never sitting still. Others can sit still long enough to fill a board with pegs, build with blocks or use large size crayons.

The following list of toys should fill your child's needs. All have intrinsic "play value" and have stood the test of time.

First Ride—on Toys

Since the ability to pedal a bike rarely comes before a child is three years old, first ride-on toys are known as "foot-to-the-floor" ride-ons. These must be well-balanced, easy-to-mount and correctly proportioned. Try them out at the toy store with your child. Put your child on backwards to see if the toy is stable even when used incorrectly. Here are the best:

Toys for Toddlers

Riding horse, by Fisher-Price, is a sturdily constructed, easy-to-mount, colorful toy. Wheels make a clippity clop sound as they turn and reins whinny when they are pulled. The specially-shaped seat has a handle backstop for pushing, and the bottom has a built-in storage tray.

Tyke Bike, by Playskool, has been on the market for over 15 years. This bike has red wheels and chrome plated handlebars with soft plastic grips and streamers.

Cozy Coupe, by Little Tykes, is a foot-to-the-floor car. It has a bright yellow roof, swivel-action front wheels, a door that opens and closes, a storage compartment behind the seat and an easy-to-grip steering wheel. It is expensive, but worth it.

Toddlin' Train, by Tomy, has a choo choo whistle and its face chugs in and out. It is a classic toy that in addition to being used as a ride-on toy can be pushed around.

Sit 'n Spin, by Kenner, is a classic ride-on toy that needs no batteries and has no motor. The child turns the revolving platform at his own speed.

Manipulative Toys

✪ **Small Wooden Blocks**, by many manufacturers, are classics. They are embossed with letters and numbers and begin teaching children to recognize these symbols.

○ **Large Wooden Blocks.** The best large wooden blocks are made out of hardwood (oak or maple) and this will be indicated on the box. Hardwood blocks will last for decades. No major American manufacturer currently markets hardwood blocks, but better toy stores carry some from smaller companies.

○ **Puzzles.**

First puzzles for toddlers should have no more than four or five pieces and each piece should be a whole picture. The pieces should be easy to lift up and put down. Knobs on the pieces are useful at the toddler stage. Puzzles help children develop eye-hand coordination.

First Puzzles, by Playskool, have large, simple pieces of wood. **Easy Puzzles,** also by Playskool, have more pieces and depict larger scenes.

Pick—Up and Peek Wood Puzzles, by Fisher-Price, have a "surprise" picture underneath the piece which relates to the top picture. Plastic knobs make the pieces easy to lift and replace.

Toddler Tote Sampler, by Lauri, comes in its own clear plastic bag that snaps. Lauri puzzles are made out of brightly colored crepe foam. Their toddler set includes simple one, two and three piece puzzles of familiar objects. Lauri's **Junior Fit—a—Space** is another early learning classic toy.

My First Puzzle and **Didacta,** by Ravensburger, are geared for two and three year olds. Ravensburger is a major European toy and game manufacturer known for its beautiful artwork.

✪ Shape Sorters

Shape Sorters are three-dimensional puzzles. These toys have a box made of either wood or plastic with a removable lid. Colored blocks of different shapes fit into matching holes in the sorter. Toddlers learn to differentiate shapes and coordinate their hands to fit the shapes into the sorter box. Several toy companies make versions of this excellent toy. Tupperware makes a plastic shape sorter with ten different shapes (shown on the next page).

Toys for Toddlers

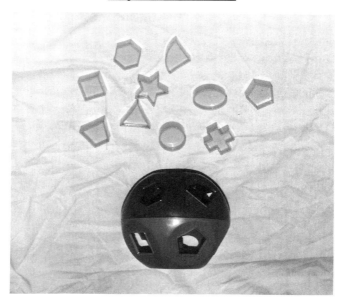

Building Systems

Building systems are interlocking toys or stackable toys that can be assembled in an infinite variety of ways. These types of toys can be played with for years. As your child develops you can buy additional pieces so that he can build more complex things out of them.

◆ ✪ **Bristle Blocks**, by Playskool, are a great first building toy. The brightly colored plastic blocks have flexible bristles, all over the surface, like a hairbrush, but thicker. With a little pressure bristle blocks interlock in many ways—there is no wrong way to build with these blocks. They come in a variety of sets, ranging from a 12-piece starter set to a set with more than 100 pieces, all packaged with carrying handles.

46

Good Toys

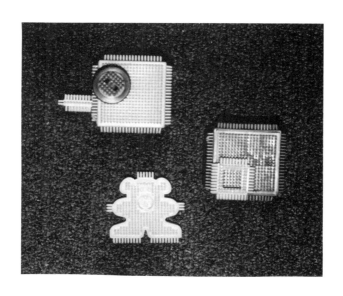

Toys for Toddlers

◆❖ **Duplo Blocks**, by Lego, are large-size versions of Lego building sets. Even though they were designed for children under age three, older children still love to play with them. They are safe and fun and hold children's interest for a long time. Duplo blocks can be used with Legos.

Large, cardboard "Brick" Blocks by various manufacturers, come in flat, cardboard sheets stenciled with a brick pattern. They are as easy to assemble as a cardboard box, and so lightweight that a child can lift several with one hand. In addition they are strong enough for a child to stand on. When assembled they are about three by five by ten inches.

Creative/Expressive Toys

Pegboard Sets, by Lauri, have giant (two inch), chubby headed, multicolored pegs and sturdy pegboards made of crepe foam rubber. Children make designs and patterns with the pegs.

Arts and Crafts

Finger Crayons, by Battat (Canada), are unique and wonderful for beginners. They are shaped like cones and pointed hats. They fit over the fingers.

Jumbo Crayons, by Crayola are easy for small fingers to use and come in nice, bright colors.

Finger paints, by Crayola and other manufacturers, come in big, fat jars and a variety of colors. They are messy so be prepared for it.

Imaginative Playthings

Chatter Telephone, by Fisher-Price, stands up to a toddler's abuse. It has wide plastic wheels, "eyes" that roll when the string is pulled, a "voice" that says "chatter, chatter" and a bell rings that when the dial is turned. This perennial favorite has been around for 25 years.

Discovery Cottage, by Fisher-Price, has over 13 features in a compact playset. A door makes a ratcheting sound, the garage door becomes a ramp when opened, a push bulb rings the door bell and so forth. Two "little people" are included. It is another classic toy.

○ **Mr. Potato Head**, by Playskool, has been one of the best-selling toys for the under three set for over 35 years. Mr. and Mrs. Potato Head come with various sets of eyes, ears, noses and mouths with which children can create funny and creative faces. The Potato Head design has recently been updated and the concept expanded. Now there are smaller-sized Potato Heads that come in playsets.

Mickey Mouse Talking Phone, by Playskool, was first introduced in 1963. Very young children can call six of their favorite Walt Disney characters and listen to a recorded message in the character's voice.

Cash Register, by Fisher-Price, looks like the real ones did before computerized checkouts took over. Children use colored plastic coins, turn a crank and a bell rings while the cash drawer pops open.

Learning Curve Fun Tote, by Panosh Place, is a brightly colored cloth bag containing a portable activity center. A shape sorter and a play telephone are included. It is part of the larger Learning Curves system.

○ **Little People Garage**, by Fisher-Price, is a long-time favorite playset. It includes a three-level parking garage, elevator, ramps, gas pump and little people. The elevator lifts cars, a bell rings, stop signs raise and lower and a crank rotates the platform to move cars to parking spaces. Similar playsets by Fisher-Price include a **Farm**, a **Zoo**, an **Airport**, and a **School Bus**.

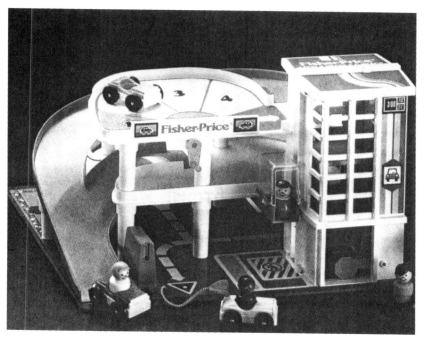

Baby Buggy, by Little Tykes, is a sturdily constructed, pink, egg-shaped play baby carriage, which has extra large, easy rolling wheels and chrome-plated handlebars. It comes completely assembled and is a beauty.

Tuff Stuff Shoppin' Basket, by Mattel, is a large marketbasket that is big enough to hold play food. It is sturdy and easily assembled without tools. It is durable and washable.

Dolls

❂ **Dolls,** Every child should have several dolls. The best at this age are soft and washable. Dolls that have eyes that open and close, that drink and "wet" and don't have any other gimmicks, have been favorites for years.

My Buddy, by Playskool, is a large, heavy, tall, sturdy doll geared to young boys. He's dressed in overalls, sneakers and a baseball cap, but also fits into infant clothing (size 3-6 months). The popularity of this doll confirms that boys as well as girls enjoy dressing and undressing play. A rough and tumble **Kid Sister** joins My Buddy this year.

Dressy Bessy and **Dapper Dan**, by Playskool, are cloth dolls that enable young children to practice dressing by using zippers, buttons, snaps and laces that are on the dolls.

Toys for Toddlers

Bath Toys

Empty plastic bottles from shampoo or soap, funnels, cups and other non-rusting household items make good bath toys.

✪ **Bathtime Water Works**, by Johnson & Johnson, is made of five pieces, each of which does something different. One squirts, one pours, one sprinkles, one floats and one scoops. All combine to make the water works machine.

Soft Bathtub Foam Blocks, by Marlon, are pastel colored, foam blocks set that will stick to each other when wet, and will not absorb water. These blocks will not "pill" so no little pieces can separate to be accidentally swallowed. A mesh storage bag is included. Some other makes of foam blocks can "pill" and are potentially dangerous.

Rub—A—Dub Magic Soap Crayons can write on bathtub tile and wipe right off. Set includes 36 crayons.

Zoo Goo is fingerpaint for the bathtub. It comes in three 4 ounce tubes of red, yellow and blue. Pictures dissolve into cleaning bubbles.

Bath Books are made by many different companies. They are made of cushiony vinyl and sometimes they float.

Other Good Toys for Toddlers

✪ One of the best hammering toys is Playskool's **Real Wood Cobbler's Bench**. It is built to withstand rough treatment. The bench comes with a wooden hammer and six brightly colored pegs. The child can bang as hard as he likes. When the pegs are knocked in you can turn the bench over and have him hammer them back again.

Pound the Ball is another hammering toy. It includes a hammer and four wooden balls. The child hammers the balls down a hole until they disappear. The balls then go down a ramp and can be hammered in again.

○ **Push/Pull Toys** are great for toddlers. They love to pull and carry things around the house. A wooden rod instead of a string will not get caught around the child's neck, leg or furniture. Fisher-Price's **Corn Popper** is a push/pull toy with a wooden rod attached to a clear plastic case on wheels. The case contains small balls which "pop" as the child walks along.

Below are the **Magic Vac**, by Fisher-Price and the **Push About Mower**, by Little Tykes.

Good Toys

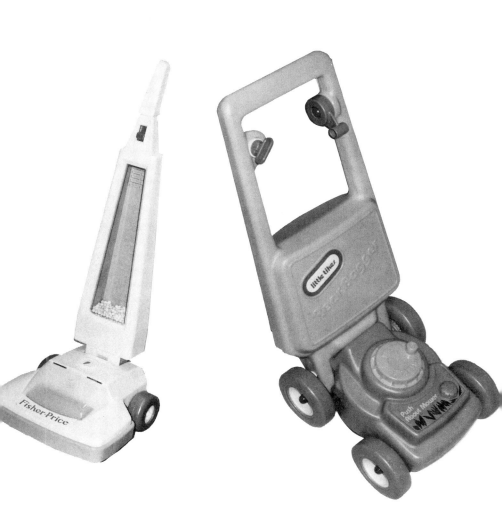

Chapter Seven

Toys for Preschoolers (Ages Three to Five)

Children undergo rapid development during the preschool stage. The toys in this chapter could be the most important ones that your child acquires. If he is attending a preschool, carefully examine the toys that his preschool uses.

Preschoolers will continue to play with some of the toys mentioned in chapter six, including shape sorters, Duplo blocks, stacking toys and the pounding bench.

This chapter includes toys for all ten toy groupings. Your child should be exposed to all types of stimuli during these developing years.

Manipulative Toys

✪ **Puzzles** are excellent toys for children. They can hold a child's undivided attention and give tremendous satisfaction. A child will do and then spill out and re-do a puzzle over and over again for the sheer delight of having mastered it. Since puzzles come in all levels of difficulty, from one-piece to 1,000 pieces or more, it is not hard to find one which will challenge, yet not frustrate, your child. Wooden puzzles are a better choice for young children than cardboard puzzles. Cardboard pieces are easily bent and grow soggy in young mouths.

The young preschool child will continue to enjoy the knobbed puzzles described on page 44. Fisher-Price and Simplex make good knobbed puzzles. There are also attractive versions made in Holland (one is pictured below).

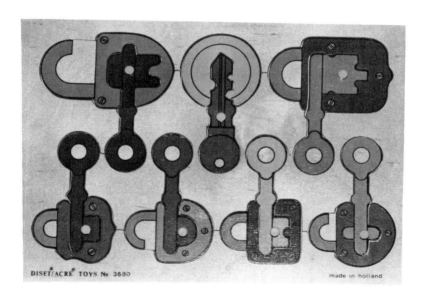

DISET/ACRE TOYS No 3680   made in holland

Good Toys

⬆ ✪ **Judy/Instructo** puzzles are well-made and offer interesting pictures to which a child can easily relate: animal parents and babies, holidays, dinosaurs, a rainy day scene, a beach scene and so forth. Their "occupation" puzzle depicts multi-racial, non-sexist views of people at work, including women doctors, males nurses, female mechanics and so forth.

⬆ ✪ **Lauri** crepe foam puzzles are also excellent and very appealing to youngsters. Their pieces are durable, yet soft. Replacement pieces are available from Lauri. These puzzles are colorful and attractively designed. The Lauri perception puzzles are particularly good. These depict groupings of animals, cars and people, each one slightly different from the others in size, type or action. Children must perceive the subtle differences to fit in the pieces.

Toys for Preschoolers

➤ ✪ **Woodlite Company** makes stunning hardwood puzzles. The designs are somewhat abstract although clearly recognizable. Replacement pieces are available from the company.

➤ **Puzzle Rack.** Once you own a number of puzzles, it is advisable to purchase a puzzle rack for storage. This will keep your puzzles easily accessible and intact.

Cube Puzzles are unlike usual puzzles. They are a set of hardwood cubes, printed on all sides with pictures. The cubes are turned to locate a particular design. Each set makes six different pictures. There are also two sided puzzles with a different picture or with letters and numbers on the two flat sides.

➤ ✪ **Blocks** are often considered a separate category of toys. They teach both manipulative and building skills. However they are categorized, blocks are important toys. No good toy collection would be complete without a good set of blocks. Blocks allow children to be creative, to experiment with scientific and mathematical concepts of symmetry, pattern and design. For the very young child of one or two years, placing one block on top of another is the beginning of his exploration of the limitless possibilities offered by this toy. By age four or five children are capable of creating structures which resemble objects in their everyday world, as well as things of their imaginations.

◆ ✪ **Unit Blocks**, by various manufacturers, were devised by Caroline Pratt in the early 1900's. These blocks are unpainted hardwood scaled precisely to one another so that the dimensions of every piece correspond to the others. The basic unit is rectangular. It is the predominant block in the set which includes half units, double and quadruple units, triangles and cylinders. Experiencing the shapes, weight and volume of the blocks is an extraordinary learning opportunity for young children. Preschoolers will learn building by trial and error, discovering how they can support a bridge or a roof. If you do not purchase a set of unit blocks for your home, make sure that your preschool has them.

◆ ✪ **Table Blocks**, by various manufacturers. Since storage of unit blocks requires a good deal of space, a better choice for home use may be a table block set. This is a smaller version of the unit block system. However, not all table sets offer the factor of size correspondence, where a half-unit block is precisely one-half the size of a unit block. A natural wood block set with proper size correspondence is made by Childcraft.

Hollow Blocks, by various manufacturers, are very large wooden blocks which weigh about seven pounds. The blocks are open on the inside for easy lifting (a child can place his arm through the open center to carry the blocks).

A very durable set is made by Community Playthings, the originator of hollow blocks more than 30

years ago. These blocks encourage large motor development by allowing children to create their own life-sized
dramatic play structures, houses, spaceships, trains and
so forth. They are indispensable for a preschool setting
but also are suitable at home if you have the space.

⬆ ✪ **Block Accessories.** To accompany a set of blocks there
are a variety of accessories that allow children to
broaden their play, including wooden or rubber animals,
people, vehicles and traffic signs.

Building Systems

There are several types of interlocking plastic blocks
which are superb toys for children and a necessary
component of a good toy collection. These building
systems provide experiences which will enhance a child's
eye-hand coordination and develop fine motor skills,
precursors of reading and writing readiness. They
encourage children to create, experiment and make
decisions. Because they lock together they are satisfying
to use. After being connected together they can be
lifted and moved.

⬆ ✪ **Lego Bricks** are the original plastic interlocking building system. This toy spans a child's growing years. For
beginners there are sets of larger-sized Legos, called
Duplos. The standard Lego blocks may be used by four
year olds and continue to see use through age twelve.

Young children sometimes have trouble unlocking
Legos from each other. Because of this children will

occasionally use their teeth to get the blocks apart. Watch your child use these blocks and tell him not to use his teeth because he could hurt himself.

We suggest that you start with one of the universal sets, and gradually add windows, doors, wheels, people and other parts. We suggest that you purchase the variety sets rather than those designed to build one specific item. Variety encourages creativity and children are often constricted by the one-item sets as they feel that they must build exactly what is shown on the box.

Tyco manufactures a block system which is similar to Lego bricks, but is less expensive. Tyco blocks are good toys too.

Bristle Blocks are another interlocking building system. They are plastic squares which connect with large bristles. Although not as versatile as Legos they fit together more easily and join in almost any position.

Snap Blocks, are wooden, brightly colored blocks, which snap together. They are appealing, but not preferable to Legos or Bristle Blocks. They are a good additional toy after you have purchased another basic building set.

Tinker Toys, have been around for over 40 years, and are a good building toy. Tinker Toys now makes a giant set which allows children to create structures large enough for them to fit inside.

Popoids, by Tomy, are accordion-like plastic tubes that are expandable, bendable and make popping sounds. The tubes fit into knobs which allow children to make spaceships, robots and other creations.

Waffle Blocks, by Little Tykes, are large (eight inch), colorful, molded plastic building blocks, shaped like waffles, that interlock in three dimensions. The set comes with one chassis with wheels. Waffle blocks also come in a jumbo size (fourteen inch) that allow children to create structures big enough to climb into. **Wee Waffle** is the small (four inch) verson.

Toys for Preschoolers

Snapland, by Learning Products, is a set of large, rugged, plastic interlocking pieces that children can use to create huge play structures. Children can play inside the cubes, tunnels and other structures that they make.

Lincoln Logs, by Playskool. These building sets have been made for over 30 years. The notched "logs" allow building of cabins, bridges and forts and teach a bit of American history as well. They are a nice addition to a train set for building a train station, overpasses and other structures.

○ **Fisher—Price imaginative play toys.** Some of the most appealing imaginative play toys are made by Fisher-Price. These Fisher-Price toys are extremely durable and are played with by preschoolers and elementary school children as well. We particularly recommend the school bus, the play house, the farm, the kitchen set, the garage and the medical kit.

○ **Dollhouses**. Dollhouses are great fun for children. They don't have to be fancy or elaborate. You can make a simple one out of cardboard or wood. A simple house with four or even fewer rooms will suffice. There are sets of little people, furniture and accessories available. Clothespin people and cardboard couches will be equally satisfying.

○ **Play Village**, by many manufacturers, is a set of painted wood or plastic houses, trees, cars and so forth. Some sets come with a mat which displays streets, parks and railroad tracks. Children can play with these sets for hours and use them with their toy cars and dolls.

Toys for Preschoolers

Train Sets. There are several wooden and plastic nonelectric, train sets on the market. Brio makes a beautiful, but expensive one. These can be used with wooden or rubber people or with the play toys mentioned above.

Arts and Crafts

◯ Arts and crafts allow children freedom to create with art supplies, paper and other materials. Make sure that you have a supply of large pieces of paper, newsprint or cardboard, as well as a set of non-toxic paints and crayons. A complete list of arts and crafts materials is on page 106.

Expressive/Creative Toys

◯ **Etch—a—Sketch,** by Ohio Art, is a self-contained, lightweight drawing box that has been around for more than 20 years. It presents a real challenge to a child's fine motor skills. Two knobs control vertical and horizontal movement and cause lines to appear "magically" on the screen. The drawing disappears when the box is shaken. This toy is extremely durable.

Magna—Doodle, by Ideal-Durham, is another drawing toy in a self-contained box. This one works with a magnetized pen.

Lite–Brite, by Hasbro-Bradley, is a console with a peg board lit by a 25-watt bulb. Children insert colored pegs into a patterned board to create an illuminated picture. Keep young children away because of small parts and because it is electrical.

Lights Alive, by Tomy, is a cross between Etch-a-Sketch and Lite Bright. This sturdy, lap-sized toy has a "magic" screen which is filled with rows of tiny holes. Using six different tools, which neatly store in the sides of the unit, your child can make designs and pictures which are illuminated by a light. To erase the picture the child slides the screen up and back and is ready to start creating again.

◆ ○ **Wooden Stringing Beads** not only provide an exercise for developing hand-eye coordination but produce a product which children can wear. Your child can also use macaroni and other pasta products with string to make necklaces and bracelets. As children grow older, beads of smaller sizes may be introduced. These may be purchased at art supply stores, variety stores or through catalogs listed on page 12.

Pegs and Pegboards, by Ideal, are made of wood or plastic. They allow children to insert different colored pegs into hundreds of holes to create designs. Similar sets include interlocking wooden or plastic gears, which are a cross between peg sets and building systems (see Georello Gears and Cog Labyrinth below).

Georello Gears, by International Playthings, is a colorful plastic design and building system. This toy consists of pegs which fit onto gears that interlock together onto base plates. A similar system called **Cog Labyrinth,** is made by Brio.

Toys for Preschoolers

Imaginative Playthings

Design Blocks

There is a category of blocks which is not for building but rather for creating patterns and designs. With these blocks children can follow and reproduce designs from pattern cards or create their own designs. Design blocks are enjoyed by the older preschool and elementary school aged child.

○ **Parquetry Blocks**, by Ideal are brightly colored wooden or crepe rubber blocks that come in a variety of geometric shapes, cubes, triangles and so forth. The blocks can be matched to designs on cards or used to create free form designs. Sets of blocks come with laminated cards that are graded as to level of difficulty.

Magnetic Blocks come in a variety of shapes and colors and are magnetized. Designs can be created on a special board. These sets are not for children under three years as some of the pieces are quite small.

Design Cubes, by Ideal, are cube-shaped blocks with four sides of a solid color, and two sides divided diagonally into different-colored triangular sections. As children place the blocks next to one another, geometric designs emerge.

Mathematical Concept Toys

✪ **Number Sorter,** by Whitney Brothers. Using the Number Sorter children match up rubber squares, containing from one to five holes, with matching wooden pegs.

Cuisinaire Rods are colored rods which come in mathematically graded lengths, each rod one unit longer than the next. Smaller rods can be combined in a row to add up to larger ones. These rods can be used for building and designing as well as for exploring mathematical relationships.

Clocks and Clock Puzzles. Judy makes a good clock with movable hands as well as a clock puzzle. With digital clocks everywhere we should expose our children to the old-fashioned method of telling time.

Attribute Blocks, by Ideal, are sets of three-colored, plastic blocks which contain four different shapes in two different sizes and two thicknesses. The blocks can be used to create designs, to match up to cards and for games of comparison. For games of comparison the "attributes" or properties of each block—thick or thin, large or small, red, blue or yellow—can be observed and contrasted. Games are included in an **Attribute Blocks Logic Activities** book, which is sold separately, or they can be invented. **Brainy Blocks** is a similar toy.

Cube Blocks come in different colors and are one inch square. They may be used for counting, with pattern cards and for limited building activities.

Exploring/Discovering Toys

These toys allow your child to learn about the world around him.

Stethoscopes allow children to hear their own, and your, heartbeat, as well as to play doctor.

A Telescope shows children the stars and the moon, and brings other objects within closer range.

A Magnifying Glass allows children to examine small details of objects, ranging from postage stamps to insects and leaves.

Magnets encourage children to explore their "magical" properties and to learn what objects are made out of iron and steel.

A Compass will teach your child directions.

Micro Explorer Set and **Binoculars**, both by Fisher-Price, are good exploring/discovering toys which are pictured below:

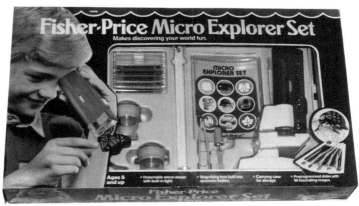

Toys for Preschoolers

Musical Toys

Tap—a—Tune, by Little Tykes, is a preschool instrument that sounds like music. This is a sturdy, well-made, colorful xylophone with keys and no hammer to hit other kids with. The different colored notes are co-ordinated with a song book that is easy to follow. It comes with a built-in handle for easy carrying.

There is a wide variety of musical instruments for children, from trumpets and harmonicas to noisy drums and toy pianos. Make sure that you include several musical toys in your good toy collection.

○ **Playing Music.** Fisher-Price makes several durable products for playing music including an AM/FM radio, a tape recorder and a record player. All are sturdy and designed for children to use. If you can afford only one buy the tape recorder because it allows children to play music and tapes and to record their own sounds. All of these products come in battery operated versions.

Good Toys

Simon is described on page 90 and is an excellent musical electronic game.

Sports Toys

No toy collection is complete without sports toys. There is a variety of soft foam and rubber balls which will be played with often. Boys and girls are now both actively engaged in junior soccer and other sports. Many children can play (indoors, if you let them) with a soccer ball, practicing eye-foot coordination.

Basketball sets. There are many junior-sized basketball and hoop sets, with the basket about three feet off the ground.

Fat Bat, by H-G and other companies, makes it possible for a very young baseball player to hit a home run. The wide and hollow plastic bat is the right size for the preschooler.

Toys for Preschoolers

Roller Skates, by Fisher-Price, have an optional wheel control mechanism on the skates which can prevent backward slides. As the child becomes more comfortable on skates the mechanism can be turned off. This mechanism prevents many skinned knees. Your child should be supervised closely when skating because falls will happen.

Big Wheel Vehicles are low-slung, three-wheeled cycles by Coleco and Empire, perfect for four year olds. They maneuver easily and are difficult to turn over. They can be noisy which may prevent children from hearing traffic. Children should not be allowed to ride Big Wheels in the street without adult supervision.

Jet Copter, by Little Tykes, is an unique-looking, three-wheeled, low slung, ride-on toy. It has a helicopter blade on top which spins during rides. Little Tykes makes other ride-on toys for children. All are made out of sturdy, colorful plastic.

Good Toys

First Games

The best games for children under five require no reading skills. There are enough other things to learn: mastering and following the rules of the game and learning to lose as well as win. Here are some good ones:

○ **Memory**, described on page 83.

Candyland, described on page 85.

Chutes and Ladders, described on page 85.

○ **Lotto**, described on page 84.

Teddy Bear Bingo, described on page 84.

Balloon Game, described on page 84.

Cootie, described on page 84.

Mr. Mighty Mind, described on page 84.

Chapter Eight

Toys for School-Aged Children (Five and Up)

As children enter kindergarten, they will continue to play with some of their preschool toys. Blocks, especially the larger ones, will continue to provide meaningful play. Dollhouses will continue to be played with, as will many other toys discussed in chapter six.

You will continue to add to some of the sets that you bought years before.

The following toys are good toys for school-aged children:

Manipulative Toys

Children will be interested in putting together more and more complex puzzles. Cardboard puzzles are fine for school-aged children.

✪ **Gridlock** is the best deal for a puzzle. It's fun, colorful and challenging—and inexpensive. All the puzzle pieces store inside a compact, flip-open case. There are about 50 different puzzles to solve, each requiring a different combination of pieces. First the child has to find the pieces he needs, and then must make them fit exactly right. For about five dollars you cannot go wrong.

Building Systems

☉ **Lego** construction sets (and similar Tyco building sets) will continue to interest your child. See page **48** for a description of this toy. You can add to these building sets. On the more complex end there is a Legoland Space Command Ship which includes more than 400 interlocking pieces and a mobile lab, recommended for the eight to twelve age group. Some of the motorized sets are for children up to age fourteen.

Capsela, by Play-Jour, is a battery operated construction set with movable gears and parts visible through clear plastic casings. The parts snap together and the interlocking parts perform a number of mechanical functions. The instruction manual is color-coded and no tools are required. For ages seven to ten.

Construx, by Fisher-Price, is unique: with its slightly flexible parts and patented snap-on, twist-off design, quick changes and easy disassembly are possible. The instruction book is a pleasure to read, it includes colorful, step-by-step instructions with arrows graphically demonstrating direction and movement.

Fishertechnik is made of durable plastic pieces which have grooves and ridges that lock together. The complex assemblies require a good deal of skill, but the child is rewarded with moving models of helicopters, pumps, motors and gears.

Robotix, by Milton Bradley, is a motorized building

system that enables the child to build hundreds of moving, humming, whirling vehicles and machines. All sets are compatible with each other. For ages seven and over.

Create—It, distributed by Wright International, is an educational construction set made of smooth plastic of bright colors. Wheels, clamps, plates and tubes press together to make models which actually work.

Imaginative Playthings

Children in this age group will be interested in playing with electric train sets and racing car sets. Girls will still want to play with doll houses, although they will want more complex ones, with more furniture. At this age the children can help by making accessories to these playthings. Children can make buildings for their train sets, either out of cardboard or wood or out of a building set. They can make curtains for the dollhouse, little dishes out of clay and many other accessories.

Paraphernalia for Pretending, by Creativity for Kids (Cleveland Heights, Ohio), makes the most wonderful set of props for children to pretend with and role play. This item was given a "Parents Choice Toy Award." It includes all the props necessary to have a pretend restaurant, theater and grocery store. It includes theatre tickets, a pad of restaurant checks, sales tags and so forth. You can buy **Let's Pretend** packets for separate activities (Theater, Store, Office, Restaurant). Creativity for Kids also makes a **Creative Art Box** and **Puppet Kits**. For ages five and over.

Barbie Dolls never get old. No wrinkles, no thick waist, no dishpan hands. Aah, the world of make-believe. Last year, Great Shape Barbie exercised more than Jane Fonda. This year she has a bed that glows in the dark, fashions from Oscar de la Renta and is a rock superstar.

Arts and Crafts

Caran D'Ache modeling clay has the brightest colors, is always soft and does not dry up. **Galt** is also good.

Plasticine modeling clay by Peter Pan Playthings (England), has a new formula that washes out of clothing and carpets. It sticks to itself without glue, and will not shrink, harden or change shape. It can be used over and over again. **Plastilin** from West Germany, is also good.

Color Plast, by Eberhard Faber, is the best clay that does dry out. It has very bright colors.

Fimo and **Modello** are the best kinds of clay if you want it to harden. Bake this clay in your oven at 275 degrees for 15 or 20 minutes. Packages come with four or more three inch sticks in several colors. For children over five.

Watercolor crayons, by Caran D'Ache and Reeves, are used with a paint brush and water. First you crayon on paper, then you apply water with the brush.

Easel, by Creative Playthings, is sturdy, two-sided, and has two removable trays that hold paint jars. It folds flat for storage.

Toys for Schoolchildren

Mathematical/Verbal Concept Toys

The Little Professor, by Texas Instruments, is an electronic learning aid with four levels of difficulty in addition, subtraction, multiplication and division. Shaped like a hand-held calculator with an owl's head at the top, the program poses different series of ten problems. Give two wrong answers and the little professor will supply the right one.

Speak and Spell, by Texas Instruments, is another electronic learning aid that is fun. A computerized voice directs you to spell words correctly. After a few wrong attempts the correct answer is given. Challenging, excellent and entertaining too.

Exploring/Discovering Toys

Suitcase Science, from Discovery World, is an unique series of toys that are easy to assemble, creative and educational. Each toy is packed in a reusable, clear plastic "suitcase" with a handle and complete instruction book. When put together each project actually works! Most popular is the **Door Bell,** followed by the **Magnetic Car** and the **Zig Zag Machine.** There are 16 kits in all geared to children four to eight and 21 kits geared to ages six to twelve. Most are priced under ten dollars.

Solargraphics (Berkeley, California) are pictures you take without chemicals, using only the sun, special paper and objects that you have collected. This toy was a Parents Choice Toy of the Year Award, and is modestly priced.

Good Toys

Musical Toys

At this stage of development children can begin playing real instruments like the flute, harmonica, piano, portable organ and other instruments. Five and six year olds will like **Speak and Music**, by Texas Instruments, a new computerized toy that teaches rhythm.

Sports Toys

Lil' Sport 7 Foot Jammer Basketball Set, from Ohio Art, is ideal for children from five to ten years of age to perfect their basketball skills.

Nerfoop, by Parker, is a terrific indoor basketball and hoop. The bracket on the hoop hooks easily on any door and can even hook on a bulletin board or be mounted on a wall. The soft, sponge foam ball is safe. It is an inexpensive winner.

Nerf Ball and **Super Nerf Ball** are all foam, lightweight and safe for indoor use. Other Nerf balls include a soccer ball, basketball, football and volleyball. These balls are easier to catch than their hard-rubber counterparts, and will save you broken lamps and windows.

Frisbee and **Frisbee Flying Ring**, both from Wham-O, are plastic flying disks that children enjoy (dogs like them too). The lightweight ring is easier to handle and is good for beginners.

Games

Chapter Nine describes good games, most of which are geared for school-aged children.

Chapter Nine

Good Games

Playing table games is a tremendously enjoyable and stimulating activity for children. Even very young children of two and three can learn to play simple games.

First Games

The best games for children under five require no reading skills. There are enough other things to find out: mastering and following the rules of the game and learning to lose as well as win. Here are some good ones:

◉ **Memory** is the name of two similar games by Milton Bradley and Ravensburger. Both games include duplicates of each card, which has a drawing of an object, a bird, a fish, an apple and so forth. Cards are turned face-down. Children turn over two cards each turn, trying to match them. The game teaches memory and concentration skills. You can play a similar game with your child using playing cards, matching the red numbers and picture cards and so forth.

○ **Lotto.** Players place a combination card showing a grouping of pictures before them. Each player turns up a single-picture card identical to a picture on one of the combination cards. Players must identify and claim those cards which are then placed on the matching picture in front of them. The goal is to cover all of the pictures on your card. There are many variations of the Lotto game available. Most of these are suitable as long as the pictures are attractive, appealing to children and the images or designs are easily recognizable. Our favorites are the "Dick Bruna" Lotto and Color & Shape Lotto, both by Ravensburger. Every child should have several Lotto games on their toy shelves.

Teddy Bear Bingo. Children twirl a spinner and match a colored plastic teddy bear to correspondingly colored circles on their board. The goal is to cover all the colored circles. There are other good bingo games for young children including Color & Shape Bingo.

Balloon Game. This is a simple color-matching game for very young children.

Cootie. Players roll the dice and try to complete their cootie insect by adding head, legs, antennae and eyes. Children also like to play with the cooties and parts without actually playing the game.

Mr. Mighty Mind. Children play with colorful geometric shapes and pattern cards. The game is similar to playing with Parquetry Blocks (page 69). Children must complete their design card by adding the appropriate pieces.

Games for Four and Five Year Olds

Four and five year olds are champion game players. They are good at taking turns and love the idea of rules. They are also fond of making up their own rules, of course, often to their own benefit.

Candyland, by Milton-Bradley involves color matching. A player picks a colored card from the deck and moves to the next square of the same color. The winner is the first player to arrive at the gingerbread house. This game can be frustrating to young children because some cards require them to go backwards.

Chutes and Ladders, by Milton Bradley. Players move up ladders and slide down chutes until one reaches the top. Same criticism as of Candyland: young children may get frustrated when forced to go backwards, down the chutes.

Hi—Ho Cherry—O. A spinner indicates how many cherries a player can put on or take off his tree. This game is easy-to-learn and teaches addition and subtraction skills.

○ **Domino** sets. Dominoes come in many versions besides the tradional set with black tiles and white dots. There are attractive wooden and cardboard sets picturing shapes, animals, food and other objects. All are played in the same manner by linking up matching images.

Blockhead, by Pressman. Players stack the oddly shaped wooden pieces trying not to cause the structure to tumble down. This game builds patience, concentration and fine-motor skills.

Numberland. This game builds recognition of numbers as children match plastic numbers to pictures to move around the board.

Board Games for School—Aged Children

○ **Checkers,** is derived from the ancient Egyptian game of Alquerqu and was played in France in its present version since 1720. At about the same time Europeans formalized the rules of chess. Both games are played on the same board and are often sold together as a set. Checkers teaches strategy and planning ahead.

○ **Chess,** one of the oldest games (originated in 500 A.D. north of India) is complex, but can be played on a rudimentary level by seven and eight year olds. Even at this basic level chess teaches concentration and strategy.

Backgammon is an another ancient board game played by two persons. It originated in Samaria about 2600 B.C. It was first played in Europe in the 11th century where it was called tables. Like chess, it can be played on many levels and is suitable for children as well as adults.

Chinese Checkers was derived from the 19th century English game of Halma. This colorful game involves six sets of marbles and a star-shaped playing board. It teaches children strategy, and they can use the marbles to play other games.

Good Games

Connect Four, by Milton Bradley, is a game of vertical strategy, played somewhat like checkers. Each player tries to build a row of four playing pieces—horizontally, vertically or diagonally—while trying to prevent the opponent from doing the same. Play is quick, challenging and uses a lot of strategy. Ages seven and over.

Pente, by Parker Brothers, is a sophisticated-looking game for two players that comes with a soft vinyl board in a tube. The object of the game is to get five sones in a row or capture five pairs. The game grows in complexity as skill of the players improve. Ages eight and up.

Clue, by Parker Brothers is a classic detective game where three to six players track down the culprit, establish the scene of the crime and determine the murder weapon. Ages eight to adult.

Go to the Head of the Class, by Milton Bradley, is an educational and entertaining quiz game of general knowledge. There are 792 questions and answers in three age categories. Players move ahead from desk to desk and grade to grade. The winner is the first player to graduate. Ages eight and over.

Mastermind, by Invicta, is a game of pure logic, where your opponent chooses a code pattern of pegs and you try to discover the pattern by deductive reasoning. This game may be played on several levels and is also suitable for adults.

Monopoly, by Parker Brothers, is over 50 years old. It's the game of real estate wheeling and dealing, where you build houses and collect rent. Ages eight and over.

Good Toys

Labyrinth Game, by Brio, is a coordination game that is built to last, made of solid wood construction with dovetailed corners. Players turn knobs to tilt the maze and maneuver a ball through the course. Ages six and up.

Othello, by Milton Bradley, is a game of strategy where you must outflank an opponent's disks. Any disks that are captured in this manner are flipped over to your color and the dominant color wins. Ages eight and over.

Sorry, by Parker Brothers, is a classic game of slide pursuit, where players have to contend with slides, backwards and forwards moves, and special "sorry" cards that can send you back to the start. Ages six and up.

Trivial Pursuit, Young Players Edition, by Selchow & Righter, is an information game that comes boxed with 6,000 questions. It requires a high degree of reading skill, but many questions are multiple choice, or "yes" or "no." A challenging, fun games for families. Ages nine and over.

Word Games

❂ **Boggle.** Players make words from 16 lettered cubes in three minutes. A very stimulating game for children eight and over.

Upwords, by Milton Bradley, is a well-made, three-dimensional strategy game with a difference. Players can form new words by building layer upon layer of letters. For example, "toy" can be changed to "joy," when a player places a "j" on top of a "t." Letters are large and bold, and interlock with each other and with the board. Ages ten and up.

○ **Scrabble** and **Scrabble Junior,** by Selchow & Righter. In both games players pick letters and form words on a large crossword puzzle board. Scrabble Junior has two sides to its playing board. On one side there are pre-printed words that children can copy. The other side is the conventional Scrabble board. Scrabble Junior uses larger letters and is recommended for players from six to ten years of age. Scrabble is recommended for players eight and up.

Card Games

Old Maid, Go Fish, Concentration, Crazy Eights, Slap Jack, Canasta and War are all popular card games with children. Games, such as Canasta, have complex rules, but children can learn them if adults teach them how to play.

○ **Uno,** by International Games, is similar to Crazy Eights. It involves matching cards in your hand, by color or number, to the cards turned up in the pile. Cards must match in order for a player to discard. There are also wild cards, reverse order cards and other special cards, so strategy comes into play. The winner is the first to discard all of his cards. Although Uno is recommended for children ages seven and up, five year olds can play this game.

Jumbo Old Maid, by Milton Bradley, is a classic game where players select a card from an opponent's hand

and try to eliminate all their cards by pairing characters. Ages five to ten.

Milles Bornes, by Parker Brothers, is a very enjoyable card game about a car race. Mileage cards are drawn and played. Players try to stop each other from completing a trip by placing "flat tire," "accident," "speed limit," and other cards on one another. Ages eight to adult.

Electronic Games

Simon and **Pocket Simon,** by Milton Bradley, is a challenging electronic memory game. Players try to repeat Simon's sequence of sounds and flashing lights in exact order. There are three different ways to play the game and four different skill levels.

Other Games for Children Six and Over

Tri—ominos. This game has tiles which have three sides and numbers that are matched up as in dominos. There is a picture version of this game for four to eight year olds.

○ Kaliko, by Future Classics, and **Trax,** by Excalibre Games. An intricate design emerges as players connect tiles to create a network of paths of two (Trax) or three (Kaliko) colors. Tiles are placed so that paths of the same color are touching. **Can You Make Contact?** and **Waterworks** involve the same principle.

Adi, by World Wide Games. The game consists of cowrie shells and a wooden board with pits scooped out into which the shells are placed. Players move their shells into other pits trying to capture the most shells. This is an old African game which involves all the mathematical complexity of the computer age.

Skittles, by World Wide Games. This is a beautiful hardwood table game in which player take turns spinning a top. The top takes off, moving around the board, racking up points as it knocks over the pins.

Go, by Sabaki Go Company. This is an ancient Chinese strategy game. Its rules are simpler than chess, but strategy can be just as complicated. This game can be played on many levels of skill.

Stratego, by Milton Bradley. Each player controls an army. The first player to locate and capture the other's flag wins the game. This game has been around for about 25 years.

Yahtzee, by Milton Bradley, is a simple but challenging, family dice game. Ages eight and up.

Chapter Ten

Making Toys

Children should not live by manufactured toys alone. Every home, and every nursery school and day care center should have a good supply of materials available so that children can experiment with their own ideas and develop their creative skills to make toys and other inventions.

This chapter should only provide some ideas for making toys and games. Most of the toys and games should be made with your child participating, or at least watching you.

Making toys and games shows your child that not everything is bought in a store. It also provides an activity for rainy days and evenings. Homemade toys are often more enjoyable to play with because your child participated in the making of them.

Homemade toys fit into the same categories as store-bought toys. Don't be limited by the toys that we suggest.

Making Toys and Games

Manipulative Toys

Flannel Board. It is easy to make your own flannel board with felt pieces. Cover a piece of cardboard with felt and secure it in place. Cut pieces of felt into shapes (squares, rectangles, circles for younger children; animals, objects for older children). Use pictures in coloring books for models. You can also cut out letters and numbers. The felt pieces stick to the flannel board.

Magnet Fishing. Find a pole about 18 inches long or buy a wooden dowel about that length. Draw and color fish and cut them out of cardboard. Attach paper clips to each fish. Tie a piece of heavy string to the pole and secure a magnet to the end. Magnets are available at crafts and hardware stores. Place fish in a plastic tub, cardboard box or on a sheet of blue construction paper. The magnet will pick up the paper clips and your young fisherman can pull in the fish.

Puzzles. Puzzles can be made out of cardboard or plywood. Cardboard is easier but wood much more durable.

To make a cardboard puzzle first choose a magazine photo or a child's own drawing. You will need glue (rubber cement, glue stick, or other), cardboard and clear contact paper.

Start by letting your child select a photo or drawing that he or she really likes—a favorite athlete, celebrity, cartoon character or personal drawing, for example. Paste the puzzle image onto cardboard carefully. Be sure to spread the adhesive evenly and affix the image slowly, from one edge then across in one direction; this will reduce the chance of air bubbles between the puzzle face and backing. It might be a good idea to paste the photo or drawing onto an oversized piece of cardboard, and then trim it.

Next, cover carefully with clear contact paper. If a bubble develops, a pinprick or small incision can be made.

You now have a sturdy picture, ready to become a puzzle. Flip it over and design a grid that is appropriate to your child's age and skill. You may want to use conventional puzzle piece shapes or invent new ones.

Older children should be encouraged to design and cut these puzzles entirely on their own. For very young children, you might want to leave a one-half inch cardboard border to make their assembly a little easier. One important thing to keep in mind for all puzzles is that individual pieces have a tendency to "disappear;" storing unassembled pieces in labeled manila envelopes or plastic bags should reduce this risk. After all, nobody really likes to start a puzzle that can't be finished! And if a puzzle becomes "too easy" for your child, encourage him or her to make a new, more challenging one.

Building Systems

Homemade Building Systems. Use popsicle sticks or tongue depressors, pipe cleaners and styrofoam blocks for a homemade building system. These can be combined with store-bought systems. Tinker toys can be connected to styrofoam, as can bristle blocks.

Easy Jumbo Blocks. These blocks are made from cardboard half-gallon milk cartons. Wash out and save your half-gallon milk cartons. Cut the top off of the carton. Tape a piece of cardboard to the opened end. Decorate and secure with colored contact paper.

Possible variations include enclosing bells inside the blocks, or decorating each carton piece separately so that the block can hold small toys or figures or trinkets. Different colors can be applied to different sides of the blocks, allowing your child to experiment with color combinations and patterns. You can also easily make extra large dice or number and letter blocks.

Imaginative Playthings

Clothespin Dolls. Use non-spring-type clothespins. Draw faces on the round top. Add yarn or string for hair. Make clothing out of fabric scraps. These make fine dollhouse families.

Dollhouse Furniture. Household "trash" can be used to make extremely clever pieces of tiny furniture: little boxes make furniture; toothpaste caps make vases or glasses; magazine cut-outs pasted to large buttons or small pieces of wood or cardboard make framed pictures. It takes a bit of imagination, but once you get started you will have a dollhouse furnished in no time.

Stuffed Animals. Soft, safe stuffed animals can be made easily and economically in your own home. All you really need is graph paper, cardboard, scissors, glue, miscellaneous material, stitching and stuffing. All parents know that stuffed animals can become endearing companions for children. Chances are that your child will enjoy a stuffed animal even more if he or she has a hand in making it.

As far as materials go, most remnants of old clothes

are just fine for the stuffed mouse and bird we're going to show you how to make. Printed cotton works best; the only fabrics you really should **not** use are non-washable ones or ones that will be difficult to sew with.

If you don't find something suitable around the house, you can always purchase a yard or so at a fabric store.

Small pieces of felt (for decorative details) can be found in any art supply or variety store. Kapok, foam rubber chips or other lightweight but firm materials work well for stuffing, as do old nylon stockings. Cotton wool, cotton balls and other cotton mixtures, however, tend to get lumpy.

Mouse

Materials:

> 1/4 yard of printed cotton or other material for body
>
> 6 inch square piece of felt for head and ears (color should complement body)
>
> 9 inch length of furnishing cord for tail
>
> scrap of black felt for eyes
>
> small piece of stiff cardboard for base
>
> approximately 3 ounces of stuffing
>
> graph paper, cardboard, pencil, non-toxic glue

MOUSE

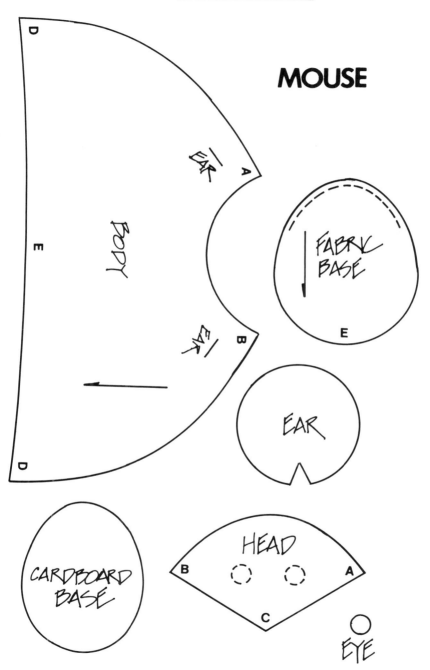

Cutting:

If you are using a printed fabric, place the material on a table with the wrong side up. Position your sturdy pattern cut-out on top of the fabric and stabilize it with a heavy object. Then draw around the cut-out using a pencil or laundry pen (or tailor's chalk for very dark fabrics). Cut with a continuous action, not short, jagged cuts. Remember to cut two eyes and two ears for the mouse.

Sewing:

Be sure to use a double length of thread, keep all stitching 1/4 inch from the edges, and finish off each thread securely in anticipation of stuffing the animal.

■ Sew the head to the body with right sides of the fabric facing each other; sew A to A, and B to B.

■ Fold the body and head in half, again with right sides facing, then sew the edges together from C to D, attaching the tail in the position indicated on the body pattern. Knot the exposed end of the tail and sew the other end into the body.

■ Attach the mouse's fabric base by matching E to E and sewing to the body with right sides facing. Leave a four inch opening at the tail end.

Stuffing:

This step determines the animal's shape, so the stuffing should be done slowly and carefully. On the whole, it's better to have a toy that is stuffed too firmly than too soft. Begin by turning the stitched fabric right side out and filling the extremities first (a knitting needle or the blunt end of a pencil can help you reach difficult corners). Insert the piece of cardboard base just before the stuffing is completed, then finish filling the mouse's bottom and stitch the opening together.

Finishing:

■ Fold each ear in half and sew the two straight edges together; then sew the ears to the body in the positions indicated.

■ Glue on the eyes and allow to dry.

Bird

Materials:

1/4 yard fabric for body (preferably printed cotton with a colorful design)

small piece of single-tone fabric for head (choose a color to complement body)

5 inch square piece of felt for color

black and white felt scraps for eyes

red felt for beak

approximately 4 ounces of stuffing

Good Toys

Cutting:

Body—cut two in printed cotton.

Underbody—cut one in printed cotton.

Tail—cut one in printed cotton.

Head—cut one in single-tone fabric.

Collar—cut two in felt.

Beak—cut two in red felt.

Eyes—cut two from the larger pattern in white felt, and two from the smaller pattern in black.

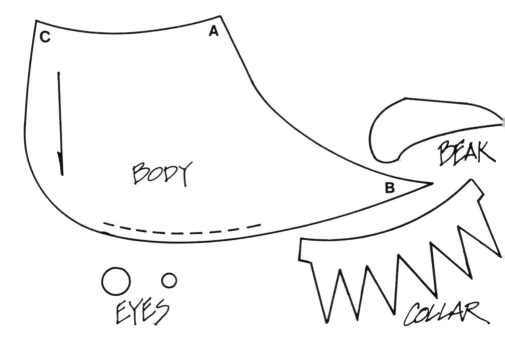

BIRD

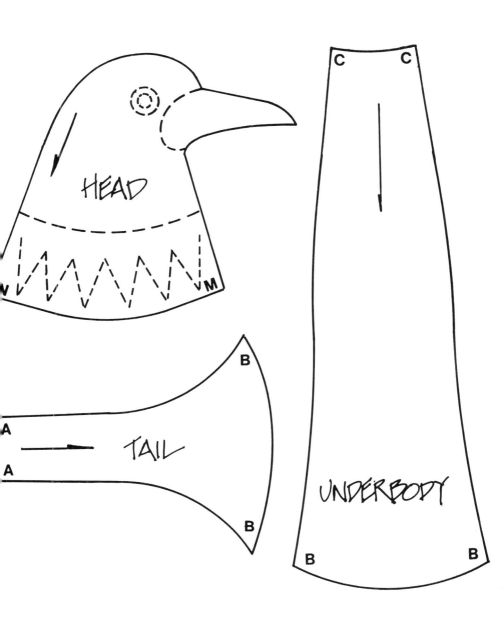

Assembly:

■ Sew both felt collar and nose pieces to the right sides of the two head pieces. Then place those completed pieces together with right sides facing, and sew around the head from N to M, leaving the bottom curve open. Carefully trim the material underneath the beak.

■ Place the tail piece to one side of the body with right sides facing, matching A to A, and B to B. Sew together from A to B, and repeat for the other side (A to B).

■ Sew the underbody to the body and tail by matching B to B and C to C, with right sides facing. Leave an opening of about three inches on one side as indicated by the dotted line in the diagram.

■ Sew the head to the body with right sides facing, lining up point M to the center of the tail piece (point E), and point N to the center of the underbody (point F).

■ Turn the bird right side out and stuff firmly. Close the opening with a ladder stitch.

■ Glue the black felt pieces to the white felt pieces to form the bird's eyes, then glue on to the head as indicated in the diagram.

Puppets

Puppets are fun to make and even more fun to use. Moreover, they encourage imagination, role playing and dramatization in children. Here are four especially easy types of puppets you and your child can make using common household materials.

Paper Bag Puppets. Use lunch size bags. The head is the fold at the bottom of the bag where the child can fit his hand. The charm in these simple puppets comes from using the bag's bottom flap to enliven the puppet's face. With a little decoration and an active hand, the bag's flap becomes animated as either eyes or a mouth. Use magic markers, paint or crayon to draw the face; yarn or lace doilies can be added for hair.

Papier Mâché puppets. These can be messy to make, so be prepared. The head should be made as follows: tear up strips of newspaper. Make a solution of white glue, diluted with an equal amount of water, or make a flour and water paste (make sure that it is not too runny). You can also use wallpaper paste instead. Blow up a balloon to the size of the head the you want to make. Dip the pieces of newspaper in the glue or paste, one piece at a time, and lay them on the balloon. Cover the balloon entirely with at least four layers of the papier mâché. Hang the head in warm place to dry. When dry prick the balloon and decorate the head. You should be able to get two fingers inside the head. Use the other fingers for arms.

Old Stuffed Animal Puppets. You can recycle old and worn stuffed animals by cutting them open and removing the stuffing.

Paper Plate Puppets. The difference between a paper plate and a big puppet grin is merely a fold. You can create a snake by adding construction paper tongue, fangs and eyes, and a green cloth glued to the top of the head. Find an old green sleeve (or sew a new one) and you've got a snake's body too.

Mini—Carton Puppets. Start with a small box from a breakfast cereal variety pack. Just cut through the middle of the box on three sides to form the mouth hinge. Draw on lips, tongue, and whatever other facial features you want. Buttons glued to small paper circles make good eyes, and yarn scraps work well as hair. These carton puppets are the perfect size for most young children's hands.

Sock Puppets are especially fun because of their flexibility: a wide range of hand movements can create a variety of facial expressions. Child-size socks are perfect. The hand goes from toe to heel to make the mouth. The top of the foot is where you place the eyes. Use felt pieces, buttons or artificial eyes bought from a craft or sewing store. The end of the toe becomes the nose.

You can decorate the mouth by sewing a piece of red or pink fabric. You may want to make a tiny hat, or cape, or even eyeglasses to further enhance your puppet's special character.

Puppet Theater. Using a heavy cardboard box, a utility knife and some simple decorations you can build a miniature theater to showcase your child's homemade puppets. Cut a large window in one side of a cardboard box. Open the opposite side of the box. Use a piece of fabric to make a theater curtain which you can connect to the box with string, thread or tape. Decorate the box and let the show begin.

Dollhouses

A dollhouse can be anything from a simple cardboard box to a complicated, realistic wooden replica of a Tudor mansion. You can use styrofoam, cardboard, plywood or foam core board to make a dollhouse. Use the materials that you have at home.

Windows can be made from plastic wrap or a piece of plexiglass or similar plastic. They can be glued or taped into place. Or a window can simply be a hole in wall.

Encourage your child to become a creative, eclectic interior designer! Attractive contact paper can be applied to create different styles of wallpaper, wood paneling and floor tile for each room. Colored felt can be glued down as carpeting, or a piece of washcloth can become a throw rug. You might even want to make little framed photo-portraits to hang on the walls. Of course a wide variety of furnishings and accessories can be purchased in stores, or you can try your own hand at them using balsa wood, fabric scraps, thin dowel pieces, etc.

Arts and Crafts

As mentioned, every home, day care center and nursery school should keep a good supply of crafts materials on hand. Here is a list of basic home craft necessities:

Good Toys

Apron or smock (you can use an old shirt put on backwards).

White glue, non-toxic.

Crayons, fat ones for smaller children.

Markers, not ones with odors.

Construction paper.

Plastic scissors.

Glitter.

Paints, poster, tempera, finger paints, watercolor.

Ice—cream sticks or tongue depressors.

Clothes pins.

Modeling clay.

Plasticine.

Play—doh (see homemade recipe, page 107).

Paper doilies.

Origami paper.

Cotton balls.

Pipe cleaners.

Buttons.

Making Toys and Games

Stamp pad and stamper.

Yarn and string.

Magnets.

Pot—holder loom and cotton loops (for ages seven and up).

Blackboard and chalk.

Styrofoam pieces (leftover packing material)

Toothpicks, dowels, golf tees.

You don't have to go out and buy all of these things. Collect them. Leftover styrofoam packing and old golf tees make nice sculptures. You can play tic-tac-toe with them or other games. Old clothespins and yarn make little dolls. Popsicle sticks and glue are good for making buildings out of wood.

Play—doh. Homemade play-doh has a nicer feel and is more satisfying (because the child can help make it) than purchased play-doh.

Ingredients:

> 2 cups flour
> 1 cup salt
> 4 teaspoons cream of tartar
> 2 cups water
> 2 tablespoons water
> food coloring

Mix dry ingredients. Add water and oil. Drop in food coloring to make desired color (here is where children can be creative). Heat over low to medium heat, stirring until firm (this is the part that **you** do). Knead to finish.

Mathematical Concept Toys

Mobiles

Mobiles are toys that can grow right along with your child. While infants can enjoy a mobile's simple color and movement, older children can learn about balance and geometry by building one.

You can use old coathangers to make the arms, nylon thread or fishing line for the suspension cords and then you can use a wide variety of materials to make the hanging objects. You can suspend dancers out of cardboard, or use old tennis balls or pieces of styrofoam or wood. To hang finished projects properly, you'll need hook and eye screws.

The key to any mobile is balance. Before you actually start cutting any wire, you may want to experiment with a ruler and coins, noting how the balance point changes with different weights in different positions.

There are no fixed rules concerning the design or construction of mobiles. The length and shape of support arms, the length of suspension threads, and the nature of the objects to be hung are entirely up to you. Mobiles can be symmetrical, assymmetrical, or even leaning.

In general, mobiles are made by assembling the lower-most arms first and adding others above them. Use the tip of a needle-nose pliers to make loops at the ends of prospective mobile arms; suspension threads can be secured at these ends by knotting, and in the middle of the arm by tying or taping. You may want to begin with a rough sketch as a guide, but much of the fun will come from experimenting with different balancing acts as you go along.

Exploring/Discovering Toys

Kites

There are hundreds of types of kites that you can build. We have included a very simple kite. If your child gets very interested you can make other kites, a sled kite, a box kite, a rocket kite or a kite that you or your child invents.

Kites can be made out of tissue paper, newspaper, plastic (a plastic garbage bag will work), nylon or other lightweight materials. The frame of the kite is made with wooden dowels, wooden strips or fiberglass rods.

To make the kite frame start with two framing pieces of equal length. Use a saw to slice a one-quarter inch deep groove into the ends of both frame pieces. Connect the pieces together with tape as shown on the diagram. Tie a piece of string around the perimeter of the frame. Using the frame as a guide, cut a piece of plastic, paper or fabric about one inch larger than the frame. Cut a piece out of the fabric or other material at each corner of the frame as shown on the diagram. Fold the excess material over the string and tape or glue down.

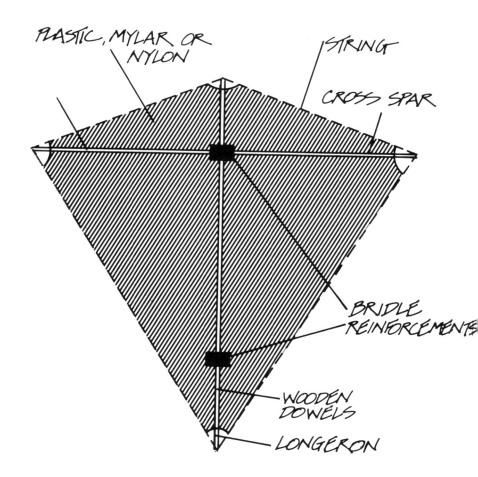

PLASTIC, MYLAR OR NYLON

STRING

CROSS SPAR

BRIDLE REINFORCEMENTS

WOODEN DOWELS

LONGERON

With another piece of string, and a four-hole button, tie a loop around the cross spar on the back of the kite. Tighten the string by looping it through the button, until the cross spar is bowed about four inches.

Reinforce the kite at the two bridle points. Punch two holes at each bridle point, or use a needle, and thread string through both bridle loops and tie the ends together. The kite line should be attached to this loop at the point where the bridle makes a 90 degree angle with the longeron.

You can fly the kite without a tail but the kite will fly better, and look better, with a tail. You can make the tail out of scraps of material.

Some kites will soar and some will flop to the ground. You will need a wind of from five to ten miles per hour. With less wind you will have trouble getting it airborne. With too much wind you will have trouble controlling the kite.

Safety Tips:

■ Don't fly a kite with metallic wire;

■ Don't fly a kite when it is raining or thundering;

■ Don't fly a kite near power lines;

■ Don't fly a kite near an airport;

■ Don't fly a kite above a highway.

Be prepared for your kite to get damaged. Bring a

pair of scissors, tape, a knife and extra tail materials with you.

Go to a playground or field that is flat and free of trees. You should not have to run with the kite to get it to fly. Have your child hold the kite with its nose up. Stand 30 to 40 feet away. As he tosses the kite quickly pull in the line, hand-over-hand. The kite should climb and keep rising. Once the wind grabs the kite, let out more line. Let your child hold the line and together learn how to control the kite's movement.

Musical Toys

Many musical instruments can be made from things that are available around the house. Here are a few ideas:

Shakers. Shakers can be made from cardboard food containers, such as orange juice cans or bread crumb cans. Fill them with beans, rice or paperclips and attach a top. If the container does not have a top make one out of paper or aluminum foil with a rubber band. Shakers can be made using the papier mâché with a balloon method (see page 103). Put pebbles, uncooked popcorn or beans into a balloon. Blow up the balloon. Put papier mâché over the balloon. Allow to harden. Puncture the balloon.

Drums. Use an oatmeal container or a coffee can. The oatmeal container makes a drum just as it is. Have your child decorate it with paper or fabric. The coffee can may be covered at each end with a piece of inner tube rubber. Punch holes in the rubber and tie the top rubber piece to the bottom rubber piece with a shoe lace or string.

A more elaborate drumhead can be made from a heavy, brown grocery bag and cheesecloth. Cut a circle out of a grocery bag, and from a piece of cheesecloth, four inches in diameter larger than the can to be used for the drum frame. Put the cheesecloth on top of the paper circle and run both under running water to dampen. Keep the cheesecloth on top and place both circles on the can. Hold in place with a rubber band or tie tightly with twine. Leave a loop for holding the drum. Dry thoroughly. Apply three coats of shellac, allowing head to dry between coats.

Drumsticks can be made from wooden sticks, chopsticks or dowels. Glue felt on ends of sticks.

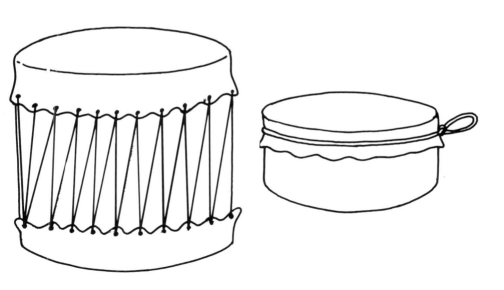

Tambourines. Tambourines can be made from paper plates, bowls or aluminum pie tins as follows: Place about 1/4 cup of bean or rice in one tin or plate. Affix a second plate or tin on top of the other with glue, staples or by punching holes and connecting with yarn.

Bottle Cap Rhythm Instrument. Find a board long enough to hold three or four bottle caps with room for a child to hold onto it. Hammer nails through the bottle caps into the board. Make the holes in the caps large enough so that they jiggle. If the caps are flattened out first you can use two caps on each nail. This will produce a better sound.

Sand Paper Rhythm Instrument. Glue or staple sand paper to two blocks of wood. When the two blocks are rubbed together a nice rasping noise is made.

Plastic Bottle Banjo. These are elaborate, but they really work and children will enjoy the construction process. Cut off the bottom five inches of a large plastic milk or juice container. Use a piece of wood about 30 inches long by two inches wide by 3/4 inch thick for the fingerboard. Make slots in the plastic bottle bottom so that you can slide the fingerboard through it, with about two inches of the fingerboard extending through one end. Tack the board to the bottle.

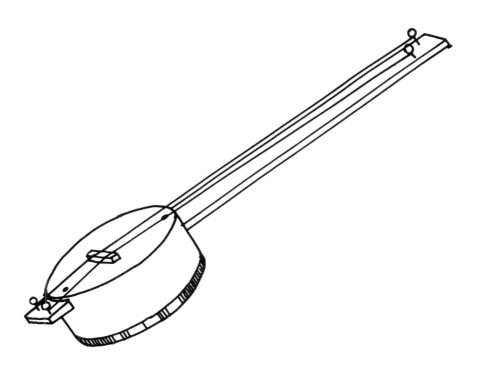

Make a bridge out of a piece of wood one inch by
1/2 inch by 1/2 inch. Cut two grooves in the wood
3/4 inch apart. Glue the bridge onto the short end of
the fingerboard.

Affix two small screw eyes, 3/4 inch apart, on the
short end of the fingerboard to hold the strings. Install
two large screw eyes on the other end of the board,
slightly angled so that they can be turned for tuning.
Tie nylon fishing line to the screw eyes and tighten by
turning the screw eyes. Test the sound of your two
strings and adjust until they make a pleasing noise.
You can experiment by adding extra strings with
different thicknesses of nylon.

Games

Knock Hockey

You can make a knock hockey game out of a piece
of leftover plywood and other wood scraps, with no
nails or screws.

The knock hockey board can be any size. The
minimum size is 18 by 24 inches. Cut (or have the
lumberyard cut) four one-by-two's to fit the perimeter
of your board. The board should be about 1/2 inch
thick, but you can use 1/4 inch thick masonite. The
sticks can be cut out of 1/4 inch thick plywood or
masonite.

Cut goals out of the center of the end pieces, as
shown in the diagram. Glue the end pieces to the board
with carpenters' glue and allow to dry overnight.

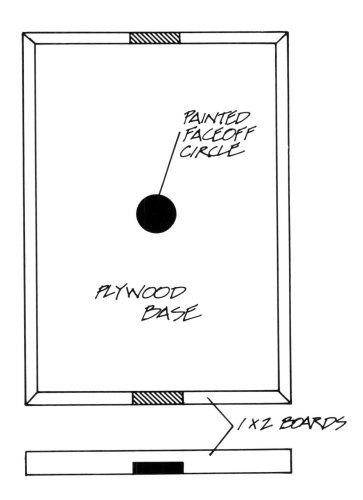

PAINTED
FACEOFF
CIRCLE

PLYWOOD
BASE

1 X 2 BOARDS

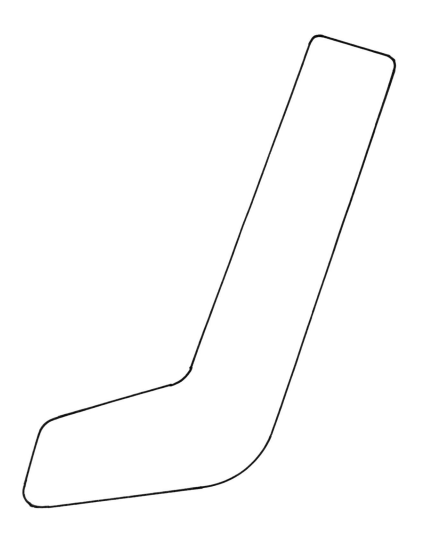

Use a round cup as a guide to draw a circle in the center of the board. Paint the circle red or blue. You will need two sticks and a puck. Cut the sticks out of wood as shown. Wrap the handles of the sticks with black electrical tape. This will prevent splinters and make the sticks look like real hockey sticks. The puck should be about one inch in diameter. It can be cut out of plywood, or you can saw a slice from a wooden dowel.

To play the game drop the puck in the circle and let two players try to shoot the puck through each other's goal. Another version of this game adds a block of wood, glued about four inches in front of each goal, so that goals can be earned only when the puck rebounds off of the side walls. Players can either take turns attempting shots or can "fight" for the puck.

Table Soccer is a tabletop hybrid of soccer—an action-packed game of skill. Children of all ages can enjoy table soccer. Younger ones will delight in the simple pleasure of slapping a ping-pong ball around the enclosed playing field; older children can practice and improve their hand-eye coordination and reaction time.

The wooden table soccer game that we've designed is very easy to make and requires no nails or screws. We suggest that you encourage your child to do much of the actual assembly, as building the game together will provide a good opportunity for him or her to learn about diagrams, dimensions and construction.

Good Toys

Materials

     15"x24" plywood (1/2-inch thick)

     two 24" pieces of one-by-six wood (actually 3/4"x5-1/2")

     eight 3-1/2" pieces of one-by-three wood (3/4"x2-1/2")

     four 28" pieces of 1/4" thick wooden rod

     sandpaper and electrical drill

     tape (gauze or electrical)

     paint

     ping-pong balls

Assembly

To make construction even easier, have the lumber-yard cut the plywood for you. Exact measurements and cuts are necessary for the pieces to fit together correctly. The first step after gathering all your wood is simply to sand the rough edges.

Next, mark and drill the side wall holes as indicated in the diagram. Now you can assemble the playing field by gluing first the side walls and then the end walls to the plywood base.

Making Toys and Games

At this point, take a break from construction to decorate the players while the playing field dries. Using our diagram as a guide, make four players for each team. You can either draw and paint the figures directly on to the blocks, or you can make paper cut-outs and paste them on. Your child can choose his favorite team colors and jersey numbers. Use a round cup or can to sketch a circle in the center of the playing field; then paint it a color other than those belonging to the two teams. You may also want to add goalie boxes and cross-field lines to add to the playing field's authenticity.

Now it's time to pull your teams together. Slide each rod through the four holes in one side wall, then through the respective players of each team and on through the other side wall. Line the individual players up exactly with your marks on the rods and apply glue with a toothpick to secure. Allow glue to dry overnight and you're all set for action.

Table soccer is a game that your child and his or her friends will enjoy from the start and then continue to like as they get better. Depending on your child's age and skill you may want to add a goalie rod and player to make the game more challenging.

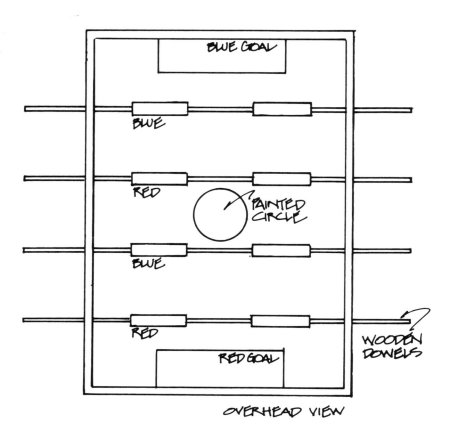

OVERHEAD VIEW

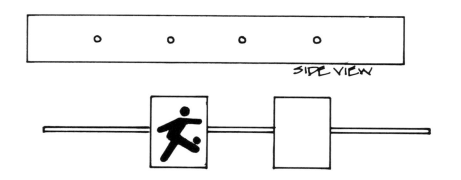

SIDE VIEW

Chapter Eleven

Toy Libraries

You can take toys home from a toy library just as you take books out of a public library. Not only are toy libraries a boon to families that cannot afford expensive toys; they give everyone an opportunity to see if a particular toy will be a good purchase. They allow you to "test drive" a toy before buying it.

The first toy library was started in 1935 in Los Angeles, California. During the depression children were caught stealing toys from a variety store in the Los Angeles area. The store manager reported the offense to the children's school principal who realized that they had no toys to play with. As a result of this incident, the first toy library was started—in a garage. The Toy Loan program was formed and is now the largest toy lending library system in the United States.

The toy library concept spread throughout the world. Although toy lending libraries started later in Europe, they have spread more quickly there. In Great Britain toy libraries are given government support. A Minister of Play has a seat in the British Cabinet.

Good Toys

During the 1970's the toy library concept spread to many countries around the world. In 1978 the first International Conference of Toy Libraries was held in London where representatives from 20 nations attended. At the time this book went to press there were toy libraries in 40 countries, and 400 in the United States and 200 in Canada alone.

How to Find a Nearby Toy Library

There are four types of toy libraries:

☐ Within a public library

☐ Affiliated with school system

☐ Independent

☐ Therapeutic

Often public libraries have a separate room for lending toys. Most libraries allow you to check out toys with your library card.

School systems have established many toy libraries, usually in elementary schools. Policies vary depending on the school system, but most school systems charge a modest fee for lending toys, or no fee at all.

In addition to these publicly funded toy libraries, in some areas independent toy libraries have been founded. These libraries usually require a modest membership fee before allowing you to take out toys.

Toy Libraries

A fourth type of library provides toys for learning disabled children. These libraries are often associated with treatment centers and provide toys as a part of their treatment program.

Any of these types of toy libraries may also have a mobile toy library. Mobile toy libraries circulate between day care centers, schools, libraries and other locations.

If, after asking your local library and elementary school, you are unable to find a nearby toy library you can write or call the toy library association in your country. The following toy library associations will locate a toy library for you:

United States

U.S. Toy Library Association
104 Wilmot Road
Suite 201
Deerfield, IL 60015

(312) 940-8800

Canada

Canadian Association of Toy Libraries
c/o Montrose School
301 Montrose Avenue
Toronto, Ontario M6G 3G9

(416) 536-3394

Good Toys

Great Britain

Toy Libraries Association
Seabrook House
Wyllyotts Manor
Darkes Lane
Potters Bar
Herts. EN6 2HL
(707) 50674

Australia

Australian Toy Library Association
c/o Noah's Ark Toy Library
28 The Avenue
Windsor, Victoria 3181
(3) 529-5848

c/o Noah's Ark Toy Library
2 Elizabeth Street
Artarmon, NSW 2064
(2) 419-2849

Ireland

Toy Library Association of Ireland
c/o St. Michaels House
Upper Kilmaeud Road
Stillorgan
County Dublin
(1) 379532

In addition to locating toy libraries for you, these associations will send you information explaining how you can start a toy library.

Chapter Twelve

Fixing Toys

Even good toys break. Pieces from puzzles get lost. A wheel breaks off of a wagon or a car. Good toys are easier to repair than poorly made toys.

Spare Parts

Reputable toy manufacturers provide replacement parts for toys at little or no cost to the consumer. The following list includes the names, addresses and telephone numbers of toy manufacturers that will replace lost or broken parts:

Brio
6555 West Mill Road
Milwaukee, WI 53218
(800) 558-6863

Child Guidance
(See Playskool)

Coleco Industries
P.O. Box 460
Amsterdam, NY 12010
(518) 843-4873

Empire of Carolina
P.O. Box 427
Tarboro, NC 27886
(919) 823-4111

Fisher—Price
620 Girard Avenue
East Aurora, NY 14052
(716) 687-3000

Hasbro
1027 Newport Avenue
Pawtucket, RI 02862
(800) 242-7276

Ideal
601 Doremus Avenue
Newark, NJ 07105
(201) 589-3000

Kenner Products
10114 Vine Street
Cincinnati, OH 45202
(513) 579-4613

Lauri, Inc.
Phillips-Avon, ME 04966
(207) 639-2000

Lego Systems
555 Taylor Road

Enfield, CT 06082
(800) 248-4870

Little Tykes
8705 Freeway Drive
Macedonia, OH 44056
(800) 321-0183

Mattel
5150 Rosencrans Avenue
Hawthorne, CA 90250
(213) 978-5150

Milton Bradley
443 Shaker Road, East
Longmeadow, MA 01028
(800) 525-6411

Ohio Art
P.O. Box 111
Bryan, OH 43506
(516) 636-3141

Panosh Place
200 Century Parkway
Mt. Laurel, NJ 08054
(609) 722-9300

Parker Brothers
190 Bridge Street
Salem, MA 01970
(617) 927-7600

Playskool (Division of Hasbro)
443 Shaker Road Blvd.
East Longmeadow, MA 01028
(800) 525-6411

Pressman Toys
200 Fifth Avenue
New York, NY 10010
(212) 675-7910

Remco
1107 Broadway
New York, NY 10010
(212) 675-3427

Tonka
4144 Shoreline Blvd.
Spring Park, MN 53584
(612) 475-9500

Tyco
Moorestown, NJ 08057
(800) 257-7728

Index

131

132

Ordering Information

You can order books directly from the publisher and pay by check or credit card.

Title	Code	Price	Quantity	Total
Good Toys	349	$5.95		
Au Pair Am. Style	357	$5.95		
Father/Son Book (Pbk)	195	$5.95		
Father/Son Book	128	$12.95		
The Magic Word	314	$9.95		
Planet of Trash (Available 3-87)	42X	$9.95		
On My Own: A Single Mother by Choice (Available 6-87)	454	$15.95		
Shipping and Handling ($1.25 per book)				
Total				

Ship to: _____

Address: _____

Please charge my credit card for these books. My credit card is: MC Visa card number: _____

_____
Signature

National Press, Inc.
7508 Wisconsin Avenue
Bethesda, Maryland 20814
800—NA—BOOKS